THE WIND BAND IN AND AROUND NEW YORK ca. 1830–1950

ESSAYS PRESENTED AT THE 26TH BIENNIAL CONFERENCE OF THE COLLEGE BAND DIRECTORS NATIONAL ASSOCIATION NEW YORK, NY, FEBRUARY, 2005

Edited by Frank J. Cipolla

and

Donald Hunsberger

PREFACE

This collection of essays is intended as a cameo view of events and people who have helped shape the notable development of wind bands in a particularly important locality during an especially significant period of expansion of a young nation. The essays are not intended as a comprehensive historical account nor are they to be viewed as the only or primary influences within the stipulated time frame. Read individually, however, they do offer a glimpse of life, be it specific persons or society in general, that has helped to mold the wind band and its literature of today. Each article represents significant research by the contributing author and the hope is that readers will find something to inspire them to undertake additional investigation on their part. The story of the American wind band can only be told by the eventual melding of bits and pieces of documented information.

The population explosion of the nineteenth century, with its ship after ship load of immigrants arriving from all parts of Europe, could easily be accommodated by the expansive facilities of the natural harbor of New York. The city therefore grew from a community numbering in the thousands to several million by the end of the century and could boast of the establishment of many fine churches, cultural institutions, newspapers, and landmark facilities, many of which are still a part of the city to this day. On arrival, a large number of individuals were undoubtedly hard pressed to communicate verbally, but for those with some musical training, that skill could speak for them and often provided a ready means of earning a livelihood. Hence, as the city grew so did the entertainment industry and a demand for concerts of all types, as well as musicians performing in theatres, on parade, in parks, on excursion boats, and in a variety of other leisure-time settings. Thomas Dodworth arrived in 1828 with his eldest son Allen, followed shortly thereafter by other members of his family. They figure prominently in the article by John Graziano as does another important name, Edward "Ned" Kendall, the famous keyed bugle player and leader of the Boston Brass Band. It could come as a surprise to find the Boston Brass Band performing not in Boston, as the name implies, but in New York on a regular nightly basis. If one's interest is tweaked, one might discover that the Boston Brass Band also traveled at times with a circus and that Ned Kendall spent a large part of his career as a circus performer, which is probably where he developed his dazzling keyed bugle technical skill. As a circus musician he was called upon nightly to perform with the dexterity of a juggler and the finesse of a trapeze artist. Both Kendall and the Boston Brass Band (which, for the record, is a separate and distinct organization, not to be confused with the Boston Brigade Band), deserve additional study. Likewise Louis Jullien, especially since every article written about him makes a point of discussing his seventeen given names plus other related facts pertaining to his formative years. George Foreman, in his article, cites a plausible but little known study which refutes much of what we know about Jullien. One thing we are sure of, however, is that Jullien was a very flamboyant individual whose influence spread to future generations of conductors, none more so than Patrick Gilmore.

The early years of the recording industry and the great contributions made by several African-American musicians is an extremely important story told by Timothy Brooks. The role of these musicians prior to, during, and following World War I, is one that is gradually gaining the recognition it deserves. Another fascinating story is that of Charles Ives. Ives has been the subject of countless articles and his music has been repeatedly analyzed, discussed, and recorded, but Jonathan Elkus captures a view of Ives and his music in a special way by relating it to where he lived, worked, and played in New York City. The same could be said for the Grainger/Ellington article by Laura Rexroth. Here we have a fleeting moment captured in a classroom setting of two giants of the music world who appear to come from opposite ends of the spectrum but have a great many traits in common from their early personal lives and their music.

The name Edwin Franko Goldman immediately brings to mind an image of band concerts in Central Park and his most famous march, *On the Mall*. Erik Leidzén also was closely identified with New York and the Goldman Band, and the relationship between these two individuals is told from a personal standpoint by Ronald Holz. Holz grew up in New York at a time when his father Richard Holz was director of the New York Staff Band of the Salvation Army, so there are many personal and professional family connections to both Goldman and Leidzén .

Finally, there is the auto-biographical article of Paul Bryan which takes us to many familiar places and brings us into contact with a number of respected musicians. Bryan continually sought out mentors who could satisfy and challenge his own inquisitive nature, a trait he successfully transferred to his students during a long and productive career at Duke University. Bryan repeatedly took groups of students to study in Vienna, Austria, not only to absorb wind music but all music and the culture from that area's rich heritage before it was fashionable for students to spend a semester abroad. He also was one of the first to commission leading composers to write for the wind band and several of those pieces have remained in the band repertoire to this day.

Frank J. Cipolla

FOREWORD

Much of the early history of the American wind band is to be found in the corridor between Washington, D.C. and Boston, which includes Philadelphia, New York City and Providence, RI. This geographical development was part of the young country's growth along its Eastern seaboard with various shipping port opportunities for European companies. A primitive system of roads grew early along with the original Old Boston Post Road starting at the intersection of Broadway and Wall Street in NYC and continuing to its Boston destination on Washington Street near the current Massachusetts Turnpike. The road traveled through lower New York State and along New York Sound through Connecticut, to Providence, RI and into Boston. Upper versions of this highway provided transportation access from Hartford, CN and Springfield, MA east to Boston.

The U. S. Marine Band began its activities in Washington D.C. in 1798 with a slightly-modified European *harmoniemusic* instrumentation. This was followed in the second decade of the new century in New York State by the development of a band at West Point under the leadership of keyed bugle virtuoso Richard Willis and then Alexander Kyle. Kyle's arrangement of the *Star Spangled Banner* in 1832 (transcribed and edited by A. L. Harstad in 1976), employed a somewhat expanded instrumentation of 2 oboes, 2 B-flat clarinets, bassoon, 2 E-flat horns, E-flat trumpet, B-flat trumpet, trombone and bass.

In addition, early band activities in Salem, MA (Josiah Flagg, 1806) and the famed Boston Brass Band (organized by Edward (Ned) Kendall in 1835) were available for emulation in other communities in New England—a prime example being the American Brass Band in Providence, RI (Joseph Greene, established 1836). In neighboring New Hampshire, the Manchester Cornet Band was active from around 1849. In Philadelphia, Francis Johnson performed with his band and toured Europe in 1837.

By mid-century, many of the NY Militia Regiments could boast of having outstanding professional bands and bandmasters. These included the 7th Regiment (Claudio S. Grafulla), the 9th Regiment Band (David L. Downing), and especially the Dodworth Band (organized in 1836 as the National Band), which was attached at various times to the 7th, 12th, 13th and 22nd Regiments and served with the NY 71st Regiment during the Civil War. These musical efforts eventually led the way for Patrick Gilmore, and subsequently John Philip Sousa, to fuse the woodwinds and brass into the ratios and balances we know today.

The band's early repertoire up through the Civil War was primarily popular-oriented with special emphasis upon songs, dances and music for military functions. A few published sources for works of this period may be found in collections by Elias Howe - *The Musician's Companion, 1st Part* (Boston, 1844), over 300 pieces of music arranged by A. F. Knight and J. H. Seipp of the Boston Brigade Band, 6-8 parts; E. K. Eaton - *Twelve Pieces of Harmony for Military Brass B*ands (Firth and Pond, New

York, 1846) 17 parts; Allen Dodworth - *Dodworth's Brass Band School* (New York, 1853; later J. L. Peters); and, G. W. E. Friederich - *The Brass Band Journal* ((Firth and Pond, New York, 1854, later Oliver Ditson, publisher), 24 compositions and arrangements with several songs by Stephen Foster. Also, several New England Civil War era brass band books have survived, in particular, the New Hampshire 3rd Volunteer Regiment (Gustavus Ingalls), the New Hampshire 4th Volunteer Regiment (George Goodwin), the Manchester NH Brass Band (Walter P. Dignam) and the 25th Massachusetts Infantry Regiment Band (William E. Gilmore). Not to be overlooked is the Francis Scala Collection, housed in the Music Division, Library of Congress which contains music he performed while with the U. S. Marine Band in the 1850s and 60s. These collections all await further study in order to better understand the development and instrumentation of the wind band, especially through the nineteenth and early twentieth centuries.

Since its inception over sixty years ago, the College Band Directors National Association (CBDNA) has sponsored and maintained research projects that have benefited wind band conductors, performers and scholars. The many committees formed over the years to pursue specialized individual subjects have delved into areas ranging from the development and proper use of instruments and instrumentations within the wind band, through conducting pedagogy to marching band techniques, and to the historical growth of the wind band. Most recently, special emphasis has been directed toward commissioning efforts to enlist today's most prominent composers to contribute serious wind compositions to the ever-increasing contemporary original repertoire of the wind band.

The 2003-2005 Research Committee included Frank Cipolla (Chair), Raoul Camus, James Croft, Timothy Foley, Michael Votta, Jr. and Donald Hunsberger. The committee decided to focus its attention upon historical developments affecting the wind band in and around New York City in the period 1830-1950, composition analysis, and recent music education and wind band development.

The essays herein were presented at the most recent biennial national conference of CBDNA, February 23-26, 2005 in New York City. They now join earlier publication efforts by Warner Bros. Publications (now Alfred Music) to further wind research through its sponsorship of the Donald Hunsberger Wind Library. Previously issued texts include *The Wind Ensemble and Its Repertoire: Essays on the Fortieth Anniversary of the Eastman Wind Ensemble*, edited by Frank J. Cipolla and Donald Hunsberger; a revised edition of *John Philip Sousa, American Phenomenon* by Paul E. Bierley; *The Wind Band and Its Repertoire: Two Decades of Research as Published in the CBDNA Journal*, compiled and edited by Michael Votta, Jr.; and, *An Annotated Guide to Wind Chamber Music* by Rodney Winther. In addition, Warner Bros. Publications also produced a journal—*WindWorks*—that accompanies the score and performance material contained in the Wind Library.

Donald Hunsberger

TABLE OF CONTENTS

Early and
Mid 19th Century Activity

The Remarkable Monsieur Jullien and His Grand American Tour *by George C. Foreman*

In his day, Louis Jullien was one of the most colorful and recognizable musical personalities in Europe. Known to his countless devoted fans as Monsieur Jullien or, simply, Jullien, his annual series of Promenade Concerts in London attracted thousands and afforded him a degree of popularity that would be envied by today's biggest rock stars. Jullien also left his dazzling imprint on America with his remarkable ten-month tour that began in August, 1853. Despite his prominent place in 19th century popular music and his role in the development of the wind band, today Jullien and his fascinating exploits are for the most part clouded in obscurity.

Jullien's Early Life ▧

Jullien was born on 23 April 1812, in the small mountain town of Sisteron in the south of France. That much is true. Most of the other biographical details of Jullien's early years come from a series of eleven installments entitled "Sketch of the Life of Jullien" that originally appeared in the London publication *Musical World* in 1853.[1] According to these articles, Jullien's parents sought refuge from a storm in a chamois hunter's chalet during a journey across the Alps from Rome to Paris. At the height of the storm, the infant Jullien made his entry into the world. During the next few days, members of the local Sisteron Philharmonic Society befriended Jullien's father, Antonio, who was an accomplished organist, violinist, and bandmaster. As an expression of his gratitude, Antonio invited the orchestra to select one of its members to stand as the child's godfather. When all of the members of the ensemble volunteered, the elder Jullien had little choice but to accept the generosity of the entire group. Thus, Jullien acquired his 36 given names and was baptized Louis George Maurice Adolphe Roch Albert Abel Antonio Alexandre Noé Jean Lucien Daniel Eugéne Joseph-le-brun Joseph-Barême Thomas Thomas Thomas-Thomas Pierre Arbon Pierre-Maurel Barthelemi Artus Alphonse Bertrand Dieudonné Emanuel Josué Vincent Luc Michel Jules-de-la-plane Jules-Bazin Julio César Jullien.

Although Jullien's parents planned to take their new son and continue on to Paris, his father had so impressed the locals with his musical abilities that the priest at Sisteron's principal church offered him the position of organist and his new friends in the Philharmonic Society invited him to become their concertmaster. Matters were settled when the elderly Professor of Music at the college died, and Antonio was immediately offered the vacant chair at the college. And so, Jullien passed his childhood in Sisteron.

According to Jullien, his early life was marked by a series of adventures, including at least two near-tragic brushes with death. On one occasion, while playing outside in the grass, a huge eagle swooped down and snatched up the youngster by his nappy. Fortunately, the diaper pin broke, and Jullien fell, uninjured, back into the soft, verdant cushion of the meadow. Another time, Jullien's curiosity got the best of him, and he crawled into the bell of a large ophicleide in his father's music room and became entrapped. He probably would have starved to death had he not been discovered several hours later after a frantic search by his parents.

As a small child, Jullien was plagued by a condition that resulted in excruciating pain in his ears whenever he heard any sort of music. Almost miraculously, the problem abated and the youngster revealed himself to be something of an infant prodigy as a singer. His father seized upon the situation and arranged a tour of the region for the six-year-old boy, who created a sensation by singing a memorized repertoire of almost one hundred French and Italian songs. Again, however, events took an unexpected turn when the lad sat down at the piano to practice one day and discovered that he could no longer sing a note. Fortunately, he had taken up the violin in secret and amazed his father by playing the opening movement of a concerto by Giovanni Viotti from memory. Antonio declared that his son would be the "Paganini of the Alps," and before long exhibited the young violinist in a tour of Italy. According to the sketch of his life, the lad also mastered the brass instruments when he was attracted to the sound of a post horn played by the driver of the coach on their tour.

At the age of fourteen, Jullien left Sisteron with his father, who had been engaged to organize and direct a band for the French navy in Marseilles. The younger Jullien was to play piccolo in the band. A year later, when his father fell ill, the son advanced to the position of bandmaster at the tender age of fifteen. Subsequently, both Jullien and his father set music aside and entered service in the French Navy. According to Jullien's biographical sketch, he distinguished himself in the battle with the Turks in the Greek port of Navarino in 1827. Unfortunately, a shoulder wound sustained during the battle ended his career as a violinist. In 1830, Jullien left the navy and enlisted in the French army. After a few months, he gave in to an urge to see his mother and deserted. But for the intercession of a sympathetic colonel who eventually secured a pardon and release from the military for him, Jullien might have spent the coming years in prison, or worse.

Such are the details of Jullien's early life as portrayed in the sketch published in the *Musical World*. Huguette Leydet, a French scholar who maintains a vacation home in Jullien's birth town of Sisteron, has written an engaging book on Jullien.[2] According to Leydet, most of Jullien's account of his early life is pure fabrication, created solely for publicity purposes. Leydet's research suggests that Jullien's parents' families had lived in the Sisteron area for several generations, and that his father was not a music professor at all, but rather a merchant. She also reports that the Sisteron Philharmonic Society, whose members' names Jullien claimed to have been given, was not established until several years after his birth.

However, the veracity, or lack thereof, of Jullien's account of his life is of little consequence. His embellished story simply reflects the personal qualities that marked his entire musical career. Flamboyance and exaggeration were Jullien's stock in trade.

The Paris Years ▨

Sometime between 1831 and 1833, Jullien arrived in Paris and was accepted into the Conservatoire. He studied with Luigi Cherubini and also became something of a protégé of Rossini, who later was instrumental in helping Jullien to secure an appointment as conductor of the balls held at the *Opéra*. Jullien's record as a student at the Conservatoire was not distinguished. His habit of bringing newly composed quadrilles, galops, and waltzes to class instead of the assigned counterpoint exercises did not ingratiate him to his teachers and subsequently Jullien departed the Conservatoire in May, 1836.[3]

By the time Jullien left the Conservatoire, he had already established himself as a conductor and something of a rival of Pierre Musard, who had introduced the popular promenade concerts to Paris some years earlier.[4] Jullien conducted balls and concerts at the *Opéra*, the *Champs Elysées*, the *Tivoli*, and the *Opéra comique*. During the Carnival season it appears he managed to be conducting orchestras all over Paris by rushing madly from one theater to another in his cabriolet.

In 1838, he was engaged for a series of summer concerts at the Jardin turc. Jules Rivière, a violinist in Jullien's orchestra, described the public's response. "These concerts, I remember, created a great sensation. They were the talk of Paris. . . .the large garden was crowded every night to its utmost limit, not to mention the hundreds of people who flocked to the boulevard, remaining outside to listen to the music."[5]

Buoyed by his achievements, Jullien eventually decided to organize his own concert venue. He leased a space, decorated it to be an appealing setting for balls and concerts, and christened it the Casino. His enterprise was so successful that he raised the ire of the theater owners of the area for drawing away their audiences. To make matters worse, Jullien insisted on programming as the last number on every concert his wildly popular quadrille on Meyerbeer's opera *Les Huguenots*, which had been premiered at the *Opéra* in 1836. The disruption in the neighborhood caused by Jullien's use of cannon and musket effects in the finale at just about midnight each evening led to a formal complaint for disturbing the peace. The Commissaire de Police served an injunction that was intended to restrain him from performing the piece late at night. Jullien ignored the court order and pushed the matter even further with an inflammatory advertising campaign. Rivière recalled: "He had enormous bills posted all over Paris, announcing that *Les Huguenots* would soon be replaced by a *Grand Pastoral Fantaisie* of his own composition. Read from a distance there was nothing remarkable in the bills, but printed in smaller type, between the big lines, were some strictures on the police and the Government, couched in most indecorous language."[6]

A warrant was issued for his arrest, and to avoid incarceration, Jullien hurriedly fled across the channel to England. In absentia, he was condemned to five years imprisonment or twenty years of exile. Jullien's Paris years set the stage for his coming rise to stardom. Not only did he establish himself as a conductor of some note, but more importantly, as a flamboyant personality as well. He purportedly fought three duels during his time in Paris, in one of which he was severely wounded and reported to have been killed in the Paris press. He also became known for his impeccable dress and memorable conducting style. A contemporary described him: "Monsieur Jullien wears a Humann [the exclusive Paris tailor] coat and fresh-butter gloves. His attitude is picturesque, his gestures theatrical, and his baton strikes the air with energy, mingled with grace. Woe to the musician who lets slip a false note! With one of his looks M. Jullien strikes to the dust both man and note."[7]

London: 1838-1853

Little is known of Jullien's first two years in London. Promenade concerts, or concerts *à la Musard*, were introduced to London audiences about the same time that Jullien arrived, and possibly he found work playing in one of the orchestras that provided these entertainments. In any event, Jullien re-established himself in the public eye as a conductor with a series of *Concerts d'ete* at the Drury Lane Theatre during the summer of 1840. For these performances, the theatre was decked out with live shrubs and flowers as well as bubbling fountains. The orchestra level, covered with platforms up to the stage, afforded the perfect setting for the promenade audience to enjoy the performance. Jullien's musical forces for the *Concerts d'ete* included an orchestra of 100 performers as well as a chorus of twenty-six vocalists. The audiences were enthralled, and the *Concerts d'ete* were an even greater success the following summer.[8]

During the first few weeks of the summer of 1841, before Jullien began his second London season of *Concerts d'ete* at Drury Lane in July, he undertook the first of what would later become annual tours with his orchestra. In early June, he appeared at the Theatre Royal in Dublin. A broadside for his final Dublin performance heralds "Mons. Jullien . . . with his "Unriavlled [sic] Band," and refers to Jullien glowingly as the conductor of successful concerts in both London and Paris. The program featured Beethoven's Fifth Symphony and also Jullien's own quadrille on *Les Huguenots*, the same rousing music that had caused such uproar at its midnight performances in Paris some three years earlier.[9]

By 1842, his third season in London, Jullien's popularity had grown to the point that his performances were now billed as "Jullien's Concerts." These performances established a pattern that Jullien would follow in his promenade concerts for the next eighteen years. The programs consisted mostly of quadrilles, instrumental solos, galops, waltzes, opera selections, and popular overtures. However, mixed in among these lighter works were more substantial offerings as well. As early as the first year of his London concerts, Jullien included Beethoven's First, Third, Fifth, and Sixth Symphonies. Throughout his career, Jullien held to his declared goal of "ensuring amusement as well as attempting instruction by blending in the programmes the most sublime works with those of a lighter school."[10]

On the "lighter" side was the introduction each season of a new quadrille, often based on a topical theme such as the *Chinese Quadrille* in 1842, the *British Navy Quadrille* in 1845, the *Swiss Quadrille* in 1847, and the *Great Exhibition Quadrille* in 1851. The best remembered of the genre was Jullien's *British Army Quadrille* of 1846, which called for the orchestra to be augmented by four military bands. Even after Jullien's death, the *British Army Quadrille* enjoyed many years of popularity.

In addition to his annual series of promenade concerts, normally in late November and December, Jullien kept himself in the spotlight with various other musical enterprises. One of the social highlights of the London year was the grand *Bal Masque* that closed each year's promenade concert series. Most years also included a winter tour of the major English cities, and in the summer months Jullien moved outdoors performing concerts that drew large audiences to the Surrey Gardens.

Early on, Jullien also began his own music publishing house. Each season, he brought out piano editions of all of the new works from his concerts. Many featured lavishly illustrated covers that are still prized by collectors today. He also published two collections each year. *Jullien's Cadeau* brought together his latest dance pieces and the more elaborate *Jullien's Album* was an illustrated hard cover book that included both instrumental and vocal works with lavish color lithographs and black and white engravings.[11]

Apart from his piano publications, which were intended for a general audience, Jullien also launched several more specialized continuing series. The most important of these, *Jullien's Journal for Military Band*, began monthly publication during the mid-1840s. The *Journal* lasted for some fifteen years, and ran to at least 158 numbers. Most of the arrangements, including quadrilles, dance pieces, marches, galops, and opera selections, were prepared by Charles Godfrey, the patriarch of that famous family of British bandmasters. *Jullien's Journal for Military Band* is a largely overlooked trove of some of the earliest published wind band music. Many of the pieces in the journal are substantial works that run to ten minutes or more.[12]

Comparable in scope to the *Journal for Military Band* was *Jullien's Journal of Quadrilles, Waltzes, Polkas, Galops, &c. for Septuor & Grand Orchestra*. Like the band journal, the orchestra series was published monthly and ran to 146 numbers between 1844 and 1857.[13] During the mid-1850s, Jullien also brought out two smaller series, *Jullien's Repertoire of the Most Admired Quick Steps and Marches, and Jullien's Music for Brass Bands*.[14] In addition, Jullien published *Koenig's Journal for the Cornet-a-pistons and Pianoforte* from 1846 to 1858.[15]

One of the most important factors in the success of his concerts was Jullien's practice of featuring many of the leading instrumentalists of the day as soloists. Most of his stars; Richardson (flute), Collinet (flageolet), and Prospère (ophicleide) are now forgotten names. However, several of Jullien's performers are more noteworthy. The most popular was the cornetist Herman Koenig, who collaborated with Jullien as a virtual partner for some twenty years. Koenig is remembered today as the composer of the still-played *Post Horn Galop*.

Also among Jullien's featured performers was the Distin Family. John Distin, the father, and his four sons were the first important performers to feature the new saxhorns of Adolph Sax. After Jullien introduced the Distins and their new instruments to Londoners at one of his concerts in 1844, they became virtual matinee idols.[16]

Two other soloists are significant because they subsequently contributed well-known tutors for their instruments. The method of clarinetist Henry Lazarus, who served as Professor of Clarinet at the Royal Academy of Music from 1854 to 1895, is still used. For brass players, the bible to this day is the method by Jean Baptiste Arban. Arban was prominently featured along side Koenig in numerous Jullien concerts.

Jullien also loved the novelty of unusual soloists. In 1850, for example, he brought the drum major and twelve drummers of the French National Guard from Paris. As the drummers played with the orchestra, the drum major preened on a platform high above the heads of the musicians while Jullien conducted. A striking depiction of the drum major and his charges enhanced the sheet music cover of Jullien's polka, *La Garde Nationale*. The French drummers were not the first manifestation of Jullien's fascination with drums. In 1846, for the premiere of his *British Army Quadrille* at Covent Garden, Jullien incorporated a giant bass drum. Later, that drum became something of a signature piece on his tours and eventually even made the crossing across the Atlantic for his American tour.

However, not all of his ventures were successful. In December, 1847, Jullien attempted to organize a season of grand opera at the Drury Lane Theatre. For his conductor, he secured the services of none other than Hector Berlioz.[17] The ill-planned project was a financial disaster and resulted in the first of Jullien's several bankruptcies.[18] Five years later, in 1852, he backed his own newly composed opera, *Peitro il grand*, at Covent Garden. The lavishly staged production lasted only five performances, and again Jullien was all but ruined financially.[19]

Despite these setbacks, Jullien's popularity grew ever greater. He was one of the first personalities to benefit from the cult of the conductor and was a pioneer in conducting with a baton. But, although he was a serious conductor, the irresistible impulse for unabashed showmanship was never subdued. He insisted, for example, on conducting Beethoven with a large jeweled baton presented to him on a silver tray. And, an imposing red velvet and gold gilt chair was always on stage, ready for the maestro to collapse into after giving his all in conducting a symphony or quadrille.

Jullien played the role he had laid out for himself to the limit, and he was a household name. His handsome features were set off by his raven hair and an impeccably groomed black moustache. His dress was that of a dandy, with coat left open to reveal a sparkling white waistcoat and embroidered shirt-front.

The journalist George Augustus Sala wrote of encountering Jullien in the course of a train journey. "I found," Sala recalled, "that I had another traveling companion here in the person of a magnificent incarnation, all ringleted, oiled, scented, dress-coated, and watered-silk-faced, braided, frogged, ringed, jeweled, patent-leathered, amber-headed sticked, and straw-colored kid-gloved." Even though Jullien had already been traveling for six days, he remained impeccably groomed. Sala continued, "This magnificent creature shone like a meteor in the narrow carriage. The lamp mirrored itself in his glistening equipment; his gloves and boots fitted so tightly, that you felt inclined to think that he had varnished his hands straw-color, and his feet black. There was not a crease in his fine linen, a speck of dust on his superfine Saxony sables, his waxed-moustachioes and glossy ringlets."[20]

Because of his charismatic personality, he made an appealing target for the caricaturists. *Le Charivari*, the popular Paris publication, pictured Jullien as something of a wild-haired, frantic figure with a baton in one hand and piccolo in the other. When the Queen announced that she did not like the polka and banned all polkas from being played in her presence, Punch depicted Jullien (who had been credited with introducing the polka to London in 1844) frantically pulling out his hair.

American Tour: 1853–1854

In 1853, Jullien undertook his most ambitious venture outside of London, a nine-month American tour. Jullien announced the project with great fanfare, and presented farewell concerts in a number of cities, including Manchester, Liverpool, Dublin, Glasgow, and Edinburgh during the months of January and February. After a few weeks rest at his chateau near the fields of Waterloo in Belgium, he returned to London. There, in early July, many of the artists who had performed with Jullien through the years gathered for a grand testimonial concert. After the concert Jullien accepted a diamond-encrusted baton bearing the inscription: "Presented to M. Jullien by the members of his orchestra, the musical profession of London, and 5000 of his patrons, admirers, and friends. July 11, 1853."[21]

On the first day of August, Jullien and his wife, along with the modest eleven tons of luggage he considered necessary for the trip, sailed from Liverpool on the *Baltic*. When the ship docked in New York on August 7, American acquaintances drove Jullien's party to the elegant Clarendon Hotel at the corner of Broadway and 38th street in a magnificent new carriage drawn by four matched horses. Just after midnight, Adkins's Cornet Band directed by Thomas Coates welcomed the new arrivals. Two nights later, Jullien was afforded an even greater honor when Dodworth's Cornet Band appeared at the hotel to offer a serenade.[22]

A week or so later, the remainder of Jullien's forces arrived. Among them were twenty-five of the principal players of Jullien's London orchestra who were to make up the core of his American orchestra. Additional players engaged in New York would swell the number to one hundred musicians for the New York concerts and a smaller, but still substantial, sixty for concerts outside of the city. The principal soloists were cornetist Herman Koenig, double bass virtuoso Giovanni Bottesini, and German soprano, Anna Zerr.

Work began immediately to prepare New York for the musical spectacle to come. Jullien and his wife, a former professional florist who was in charge of decorations for

Jullien's London concerts, directed the transformation of Castle Garden, New York's largest concert venue, into an appropriate setting for the upcoming performances.[23] As the decorators began their work, public anticipation was fueled by newspaper accounts of the dramatic changes at Castle Garden. The *Mirror* proclaimed "The public may expect something dazzling," and the hall "is to be transformed into a second Aladdin's palace."[24]

Throughout the city and beyond, Jullien's publicists plastered any available space with red and black posters announcing the coming concerts, prompting one New York newspaper to note that "every wall, brick pile, omnibus, car, pavement, and bar room in New York has been red with the bills of Jullien."[25] He filled the amusement columns of the city's papers with announcements and emblazoned his name in huge letters on the side of Castle Garden in order to attract the attention of passengers on passing steamboats. Apparently, among the eleven tons of luggage he had brought from London was the huge bass drum used in the performances of his *British Army Quadrille* some years earlier. The drum's case stood near the door of Castle Garden, open just enough to capture the interest of passersby with a glimpse of the gargantuan instrument inside.[26]

At last, on Monday evening, August 29, Jullien began his New York concerts in Castle Garden amid wreaths of roses, baskets of colorful flowers, brilliant banners hung throughout the hall, and a huge star outlined by gaslights. His red upholstered podium outlined in gold and his signature gilded chair stood in the midst of the orchestra. Commencing with the Overture to *Der Freischütz*, the program also included movements from Beethoven's "Pastoral" and Mendelssohn's "Scotch" Symphonies; a liberal helping of Jullien's waltzes, polkas, and quadrilles; and brilliant displays by the soloists. The audience was enthralled. And, despite the promotional circus that surrounded the concert, the critics were also almost universally exuberant in their praise.

Richard Grant White, music critic and coeditor of the *Courier and Enquirer* wrote: "Monsieur Jullien, having blazoned himself and his principal artists in infernal scarlet and black all over the town for some months . . . having issued an infinite series of portraits of himself . . . having occupied (and handsomely paid for) a large portion of valuable space in our columns and those of our principal contemporaries . . . having had six advertisements daily in every journal . . . having announced that the well-beloved Castle Garden of the New Yorkers could be formed into the most perfect *salle de concert* in the world' . . . having done all this, he sends us a vast and ponderous card of admission printed in scarlet and gold in the folio form, upon brilliantly enameled board, and bound in crimson morocco. . . . [All] this was humbug. [But,] Monsieur gave us all he promised us, and more."[27] Jullien had captivated White, along with the rest of New York City.

At his seventh New York concert, on September 5, Jullien introduced his newly composed *American Quadrille*. Incorporating several American melodies, including "Our Flag Is There," "The Old Folks at Home," "Land of Washington," "Hail to the Chief," and "Yankee Doodle," the *American Quadrille* proved to be a triumph and was performed on virtually every one of his concerts during the coming nine months. A reporter for the *Brooklyn Eagle* wrote, "The success of the American quadrilles is the talk of the town."[28] Featuring virtuoso solo sections for twenty of the orchestra's leading performers, the quadrille was Jullien at his best . . . showy and exaggerated, but at the same time founded firmly on the virtuosic musicianship of his performers. The *Eagle* continued: "There is more fun and more of the ludicrous in those candenzas [sic] that separate [this] symphony from the air of 'Hokee, pookie, wangi, funim' than in any music we have ever heard, and it never fails to produce a hearty burst of applause from the audience.'[29]

Even normally severe and restrained critics such as C. M. Cady, editor of the *Musical Review and Choral Advocate*, were caught up in the enthusiasm. Cady wrote that when the grand treatment of "Yankee Doodle" finally ends triumphantly, "a scene of the wildest enthusiasm follows. The ladies in the audience wave their handkerchiefs and the gentlemen swing their hats and shout and stamp 'till it is repeated."[30]

Jullien also brought out a number of other works during his stay in America,[31] among which were the *American Polka* (which, like the *American Quadrille*, featured a number of familiar American tunes, including "Buffalo Gals," "Lucy Neal," and "Old Dan Tucker") and the *Katy-did Polka*, subtitled "Souvenirs of Castle Gardens." The first American version of the *Katy-did Polka* reprinted a lengthy letter supposedly sent to Jullien from Staten Island on October 3, 1853, by a music lover named Amico who had happened to drift by Castle Garden in his small boat as the orchestra was playing. Floating a bit further on, the letter explains, the sound of the music faded away, replaced by the melodies of nature's "orchestra". . . the tree toad, the bull frog, the locust, the cricket, and "that most mysterious of all mysterious little creatures," the katydid. Returning a few nights later, the correspondent discovers that Jullien and his orchestra have gone. And so, too, have the sounds of the creatures that enthralled him before. "I listened in vain. Summer was gone, they were silent, - where too was the Katy-did? * * * Dead!"[32] Amico calls on Jullien imploringly to set his impressions to music. Jullien was, apparently, moved to immediate action, and the orchestra gave its first performance of the *Katy-did Polka* on October 7, just four days after the date on the letter from Amico. The percussionists of the orchestra imitated the sound of the katydid with a special machine purportedly designed by Jullien himself for the purpose.[33]

After giving forty-one concerts in New York, Jullien and his forces departed the city in late October for performances in the northeast, most importantly in Boston, where he gave more than a dozen concerts. A correspondent to the *New York Times* gave a glowing report of Jullien's success in Boston, "Mons. Jullien has been drawing large houses at the Music Hall, and charming all ears with tempests of sweet and magnificent sounds. If there is a musical taste in this city, it is awakened now or never."[34] On Sunday, November 6, Jullien departed from his usual program and joined forces with Boston's Mendelssohn Choral Society for a Grand Sacred Concert that included works by Mendelssohn, Rossini, and Handel.

In early December, he was back in New York for another month of concerts there, this time at the Metropolitan Hall. Although poor weather hampered attendance at several of the December concerts,[35] the performances continued to attract favorable notice from the press. On Christmas Eve, the program included the premiere of the *Santa Claus Symphony* by the American composer William Henry Fry. The final concert of the series, on January 4, drew a large audience, and following the performance the New York musicians of the orchestra presented Jullien with a large engraved silver salver.[36] Jullien announced that he would proceed to Boston for two weeks of concerts in that area, and then return to New York for a grand dress ball prior to departing for an extended tour of the principal cities of the South.

Although Jullien must have planned the southern tour to take the orchestra away from the rigors of winter in the north, the travelers did not succeed without difficulties. An ice-bound Susquehanna River almost proved their undoing. A member of the orchestra described the scene in a letter to London: "The river was a mass of floating ice, and the steamer could not take [us] across to Baltimore, where [we] were to play that evening. It was decided to cross on foot, and a fiddler volunteered to act as pioneer. A sledge was improvised for the ladies and hauled across. . . . The orchestral luggage was loaded into three boats mounted on rollers, all except the monster drum, which had to be taken out of its case and rolled across. . . . All the musicians armed themselves with huge poles to pick the way, except little Collinet the flageolet player, who could not be prevailed on any account to make the attempt. Consequently, we had to seize him by main force, strap him on a violoncello case, and have him pulled across.[37] Eventually, the tour reached as far south as New Orleans with stops in Washington, Cincinnati, Mobile, Charleston, and other major cities. Throughout the tour Jullien's theme was "Music for the Million."[38]

By early May, Jullien had made his way back to Boston. He gave his Farewell Concert there on May 12. Among the pieces now featured on the program was his newly composed *Farewell Waltz: Adieu to America*. A broadside advertising the Boston concert on May 11 described the piece as his last gesture prior to returning to Europe to "fulfil [sic] his engagements in London and Paris."[39] But, Jullien was not quite finished with America.

Leaving Boston, Jullien returned to New York for ten more "Farewell" Concerts at Castle Garden, where his American visit had begun nine months earlier. Once again, he captured the imagination of the city. Near the end of the series, a writer for the *New York Times* mused:

"When the current week is ended we may as well break our Opera-Glasses and grow domestic. What more will it be worth our eyesight to dwell on in concert rooms? The grand Jullien leaves us. We see other vests as irreproachable, perhaps at the Crystal Palace; we shall see with returning of winter, snow-drifts as white as those gloves; another imperial as faultless may reach us from classic Italy; but that air, that swaying wave of the baton-grasping hand, that total abandon when the victory is achieved - when shall that be restored to us? Oboes and ophicleides, cornets and castanets will remain, but they will seem only like bones and toot-horns, and mere cunningly-crooked wind instruments of brass, in the comparison."[40]

And, the Mons. had still one more trick up his sleeve. As his Castle Garden concerts came to a close, Jullien announced his most grandiose American spectacle of all. For this extraordinarily audacious project, Jullien took on a new partner . . . the king of humbug, P. T. Barnum. Together, they would offer a series of concerts called the Grand Musical Congress, to be presented at the recently finished Crystal Palace.[41] A large stage designed to accommodate more than 1,500 performers was erected under the dome of the gigantic building. The orchestra was increased to number 500 players. A thousand voice chorus would draw together singers not only from New York, but also from Boston, Hartford, New Haven, Providence, Buffalo, Syracuse, Philadelphia and other cities. Additional color was to be added by the participation of Dodworth's Band and Bloomfield's United States Military Band.

The press estimated the audience at the opening concert of the series on June 15 to be as many as 40,000. The program featured the *Hallelujah Chorus,* the *William Tell Overture,* and Jullien's new *Fireman's Quadrille.* Dedicated to the firemen of New York City, the latter piece incorporated the services of the two military bands and featured special effects intended to create the impression that the Crystal Palace itself was on fire. In addition to statements in the program that the fire was not real, P. T. Barnum personally addressed the audience before the piece was played. He assured the multitude of spectators that "the frightful effects that would be introduced" were not cause for alarm, and everyone was perfectly safe.[42]

Although the weeklong series of concerts produced great excitement in the press, the venture was not musically or financially successful.[43] With only a day and a half of rehearsal time for the 1,500 performers, the music was certainly less than polished. And, the acoustics in the Crystal Palace were abysmal. After the first day, attendance declined steadily despite reduced ticket prices. However, at the final performance of the series, on June 26, the Crystal Palace was full once again. Promoted as a farewell benefit for Jullien, some observers estimated that the audience was even larger than for the opening concert of the Congress. As the evening drew to a close, cornetist Herman Koenig played Jullien's waltz *Adieu to America* for the last time on these shores. Then, composer William Henry Fry came forward and after laudatory remarks presented Jullien a golden wreath inscribed: "Laureate to Jullien from 1,500 performers at the First Musical Congress in America and upwards of 30,000 of his warmest friends and admirers present at the Crystal Palace, New York. June 15, 1854."[44]

And so ended Jullien's American journey. He sailed for Liverpool two days after the last Crystal Palace concert. During his time here, Jullien had performed 105 concerts in New York City and 214 in all.

London: 1854-1859

Back in London, Jullien returned to his familiar pattern of annual promenade concerts. In 1856, he became involved in a venture with the Surrey Garden Company to exploit the gardens as a location for musical entertainments. Included in the scheme was a grand new hall constructed on the grounds of the gardens. Concert audiences of up to 10,000 listeners could be accommodated in the hall. Despite initial successes, the venture ultimately failed, and Jullien was once again left bankrupt.[45] Perhaps even more disastrous for Jullien was the great fire that destroyed the Covent Garden Theatre on March 5, 1856. Virtually Jullien's entire library of manuscript arrangements was destroyed in the conflagration.[46]

Jullien gave his last concerts in London in late 1858. Already, it was apparent that he was declining mentally. He advertised the season as "Jullien's Farewell before his departure on a Universal Musical Tour through every city and capital of Europe, America, Australia, the Colonies, and civilized towns of Asia and Africa, accompanied by the elite of his orchestra and other artists, *savants*, and men of letters, being the nucleus of a Society already formed, under the title of Society of Universal Harmony."[47] After the London concerts, Jullien made his Farewell Tour to the principal English cities, and then he dropped out of sight for several months.

In early 1860, Jullien resurfaced in Paris, where he was said to be trying to organize a series of oratorio concerts. Apparently, he was sinking into a darker and darker depression, and in late February he showed signs of a mental breakdown. Various reports had him driving about Paris in an open carriage, stopping to play his piccolo, and declaring to any who would listen that he would soon be presenting a series of concerts. Some sources indicate that he may have attempted suicide. In the end, he was confined to an asylum and died on March 14, 1860.[48]

Jullien's Influence on American Bands

Although several bands in the New York area, and probably elsewhere, included his music on their programs during the mid-19th century, Jullien's influence on the development of American bands can be traced primarily through P. S. Gilmore, who is often called the "Father of the American Concert Band." Gilmore was living in Boston during the first half of 1854 when Jullien performed there numerous times. Although actual documentation has not surfaced, without doubt Gilmore would have been fully aware of Jullien and more than likely attended one or more of his Boston performances. Gilmore certainly developed an overwhelming urge to produce the same sort of "monster" events that were Jullien's forte. Gilmore's prospectus for his 1869 National Peace Jubilee rings with echoes of the descriptions of Jullien's Grand Musical Congress in New York's Crystal Palace. [49]

Gilmore programmed Jullien's music on his concerts throughout his years in New York, even as long as three decades after Jullien's American tour. For example, the program for the concert by Gilmore's Band at Manhattan Beach on August 18, 1892, contains a work by Jullien listed as *Polka Militaire - "Drummers to the Front"* that featured the band and also the 22nd Regiment Drum Corps.[50] Quite possibly, this piece was actually Jullien's *Garde Nationale Polka* that had caused such a stir with the twelve Parisian drummers in London in 1856.

For his "Jubilee" concerts at the end of each Manhattan Beach season, Gilmore was particularly fond of featuring Jullien's music. For the 1886 season, he announced "Jullien's *British Army Quadrille,* in which Gilmore's Superb Band, Greatly Augmented, Assisted By Extra Military Band, Twenty-Second Regiment Drum Corps, and Company of Scottish Pipers, [and] 300 Troops will take part in this soul-stirring Spectacular. Come and see the Stars and Stripes saluted by the Nations of Europe."[51] Beginning in 1887, and continuing for several seasons, he featured Jullien's *Quadrille of All Nations*.[52] For the 1889 Jubilee, the press reported, "Julien [sic] played it a thousand nights in London, but Gilmore first introduced it on this side, and alone possesses the score."[53] Gilmore also programmed the *Quadrille of All Nations* on his tours.[54]

At least one of Gilmore's disciples also carried on the tradition. In 1887, Frederick Innes, the former virtuoso trombone soloist of Gilmore's Band turned bandmaster, announced his intention to form his own band to be based in San Francisco. In a letter to The *Metronome* magazine, Innes detailed how the feature of his projected concerts would be a spectacular production of Jullien's *Quadrille of All Nations*, complete with a chorus of 150 voices, several bands dressed in various national costumes, a drum corps, and a woman representing the Goddess of Liberty rising in the finale on the outstretched wing of an eagle in front of a huge American flag.[55] Jullien would have loved it!

Postscript ▣

In May, 1880, a new concert venue named the Metropolitan Music Hall opened its doors at Broadway and 41st Street in New York. Praised by the press as "one of the finest establishments of the kind in the world," the hall was decorated with plants, flowers, and statuary and featured a broad promenade that encircled the entire ground floor. The management engaged a large orchestra under the leadership of an aspiring young conductor named Rudolph Aronson to provide entertainments consisting of both light and classical selections each evening.[56]

In July, Aronson announced that he would give a series of Jullien concerts, and the orchestra would perform music by Jullien that he had just received from England.[57] And so, once again, a quarter of a century after Jullien's American tour, his music would to be heard in this country in a setting such as he might have arranged himself. For those old enough to remember Jullien's own performances here, the appeal was immediate. One critic observed that Aronson's concerts drew out in force "the old veterans who . . . remembered when Broad street was the Fifth avenue of the city and the Castle Garden the swell theatre." They were the ones who remembered that the "famous Jullien was the leader at the Castle Garden concerts in 1854, and the fashion of the town made up his audiences." The writer called the opening performance of the series "decided success, the pieces being given very spiritedly by the orchestra, and the large audience present were apparently much pleased with the novel entertainment."[58]

Aronson's programs included the *English Quadrilles,* the *Sleigh Polka,* the *Prima Donna Waltz,* and other works by Jullien. The concert reviewer urged the younger audience members who were unfamiliar with Jullien's music to seek those pieces out. "Your mother or grandmother," he wrote, "has them all bound in that square volume entitled 'Piano Forte Selections' and she will undoubtedly be happy to bring them out once more from their dusty corner behind the piano."[59] Those old bound volumes of sheet music are still around, now in dusty corners of antique shops and used book stores. And, that is where one may find the music of Jullien today (or more likely, through the current equivalent of prowling those quaint little shops . . . an eBay search).

But, for the most part, the world has forgotten Jullien. Even musicians no longer remember that he played an important role in nurturing a popular appreciation of concert music through his London promenade concerts; that he set America on its ear with his tour of this country; and that he influenced the pioneers of the American concert band. Overlooked today, yes, but he is a figure who deserves notice and further study.

The young Jullien, early 1840s.
(Engraving published by the music publisher Wessel & Co. London. Author's collection)

Broadside for Jullien's concert at the English Opera House on Saturday, December 17, 1842. (Author's collection.)

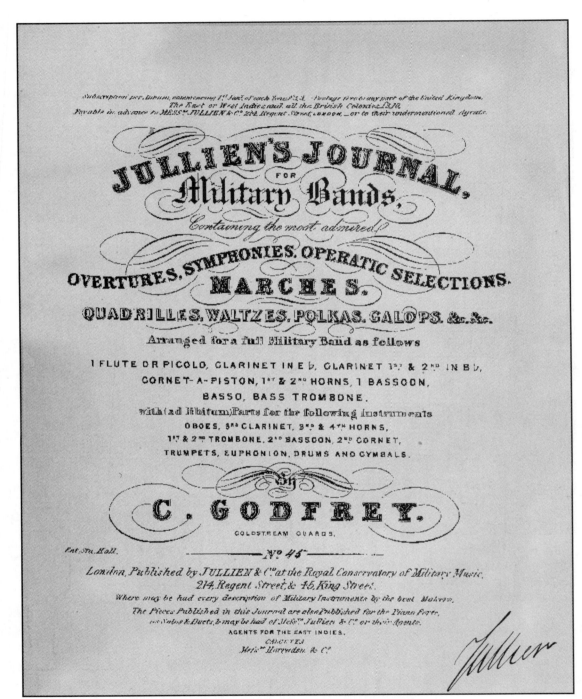

Jullien's *Journal for Military Bands*, published from 1844 to 1859.
(Brititsh Library)

Jullien with his orchestra and military bands in a performance of the
British Army Quadrille **at Covent Garden in 1846.**
(The Illustrated London News, 7 November 1846. Author's collection.)

New York's Crystal Palace, ca. 1853.
(Engraving published by Casilear, Capewell, and Kimmel. Author's collection.)

The interior of Castle Garden at the time of Jenny Lind's first American concert in 1850.
(Lithograph by Currier and Ives.)

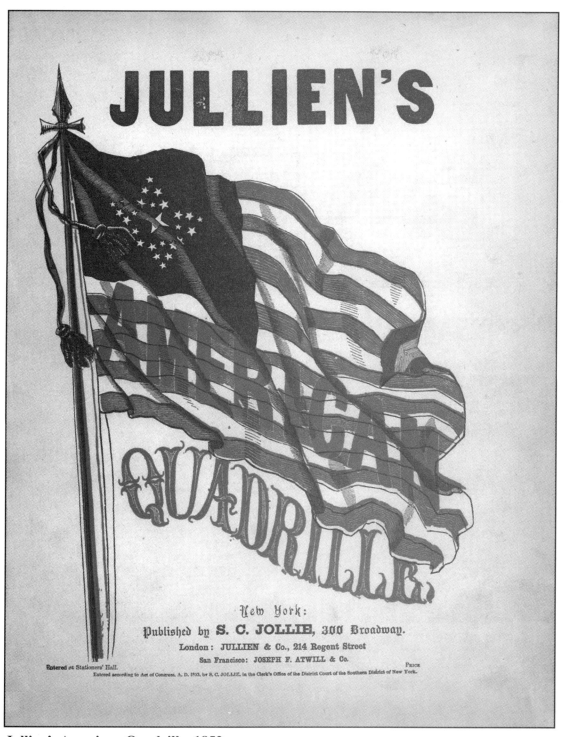

Jullien's American Quadrille, 1852.
(Author's collection.)

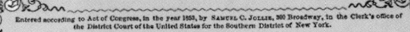

PROGRAMME

OF

JULLIEN'S

GRAND SACRED CONCERT,

THIRTEENTH IN BOSTON, AND SIXTY-SECOND IN AMERICA,

AT THE BOSTON MUSIC HALL,

On SUNDAY Evening, Nov. 6th, 1853.

Part I.

Selection from Mendelssohn's Oratorio, "Elijah." . . . . . .

1.—INTRODUCTION. 2.—Recitative and Air, "If with all your hearts," Bassoon Solo, Mr. Hardy. 3.—"Hear us, Baal," full Orchestra. 4.—Air, "Is not his word like a Fire," Ophecleide Solo, Mr Hughes. 5.—Air, "Then shall the righteous shine forth," Cornet a Piston Solo, Herr Koenig. 6.—Finale, "Thanks be to God," Full Orchestra. 7.—Air, "Hear Ye Israel." Mdlle Anna Zerr.

The Canto Fermo of the Greek Creed and Fugue, ... JULLIEN
The Prayer from "Mosè in Egitto," . . . . ROSSINI

FULL ORCHESTRA, assisted by the

MENDELSSOHN CHORAL SOCIETY.

Part II.

Grand Selection from Rossini's "Stabat Mater." . . . . . .

1.—INTRODUCTION, by Full Orchestra. 2.—Air, "Pro Peccatis," Ophecleide Solo, Mr. Hughes. 3.—Air, "Cujus Animum," Cornet a Piston Solo, Herr Koenig.

Instrumental Description of Chaos from Haydn's Oratorio of "The Creation."

Grand Selection from Handel's Oratorio, "The Messiah." . . . . .

1.—OVERTURE by Full Orchestra. 2.—Air, "Comfort Ye my People," Solo Cornet, Herr Koenig. 3.—Chorale, "Glory to God," Full Orchestra. 4.—Grand Chorus, "For unto us a Child is Born," by the MENDELSSOHN CHORAL SOCIETY. 5.—Grand Chorus, "Hallelujah," by the Mendelssohn Choral Society.

Conductor, . . M. Jullien.

JULLIEN'S MUSIC.

AND MAY BE HAD IN THE HALL.

Opening page of the program for Jullien's sixty-second performance in America, the Grand Sacred Concert in Boston on Sunday, November 6, 1853.

(Author's collection.)

Jullien's *Katydid Polka* or *Souvenirs of Castle Gardens*. **With several figures added to the foreground, the cover illustrations of the edition published by Jullien in London in 1854 was an unacknowledged copy of the Currier and Ives print,** *The Battery, New York* **(1850).** (Author's collection)

New York's Castle Garden, where Jullien opened his American tour in August, 1853.
(Lithograph published by D.T. Valentine, 1852. Detail. Author's collection.)

The last portrait of Jullien, 1860. (Engraving by D.J. Poun. Published as a supplement to the *Illustrated News of the World*. Author's collection.)

NOTES

[1] Jullien's early life as portrayed in "Sketch of the Life of Jullien," *Musical World* (May, June, and July, 1853), is discussed in more detail in Adam Carse, *The Life of Jullien: Adventurer, Showman-Conductor and Establisher of the Promenade Concerts in England, together with a history of those Concerts up to 1895* (Cambridge: W. Heffer & Sons Ltd., 1951), 18-28.

[2] Huguette Leydet, *Louis Jullien: Itinéraire musical de Sisteron au Nouveau Monde* (Sisteron: Imprimerie Nouvelle Sisteron, 2001).

[3] Carse, *Life of Jullien*, 29-31.

[4] *Musical World* (5 August 1836) reported that Musard's "praiseworthy ingenuity" in presenting popular concerts had been "overwhelmed by his antagonist [Jullien]." Quoted in Carse, *Life of Jullien*, 32.

[5] Jules Rivière, *My Musical Life and Recollections* (London: Sampson, Low, Marston & Company, 1893), 42-43.

[6] Ibid., 45.

[7] *Musical World* (3 June 1836). Quoted in Carse, *Life of Jullien*, 32.

[8] Carse, *Life of Jullien*, p. 39.

[9] Broadside announcement for performance on Saturday, 5 June 1841 at the Theatre Royal in Dublin. Author's collection.

[10] *Illustrated London News,* 10 November 1850. Quoted Carse, *Life of Jullien*, 66.

[11] According to the *Catalogue of Printed Music in the British Library to 1980* (London: K. G. Saur, 1984), vol. 32, 113, *Jullien's Album* was published for the years of 1847 to 1857. *Jullien's Cadeau* had a shorter life of four years, from 1854 to 1857.

[12] A number of pieces from the *Journal for Military Band* (American Polka, American Quadrille, Atlantic Galop, Drum Polka, Echo Du Mont Blanc Polka, La Prima Donna Waltz, all by Jullien; and two by Herman Koenig, Post Horn Galop, and Trumpet Polka) are now available in modern editions from Zephyrwind music.com.

[13] *Catalogue of Printed Music in the British Library*, vol. 32, 116.

[14] Both of the smaller band series are listed in advertisements included with issue No. 122 of *Jullien's Orchestra Journal*, which appeared in 1854. At that time *Jullien's Repertoire of the Most Admired Quick Steps and Marches* included thirty-four titles arranged by J. Mohr. The listing for *Jullien's Music for Brass Bands* included four numbers containing a total of ten titles, all arranged by J. G. Jones, Bandmaster of the 16th Lancers. The ads for both series indicate "To Be Continued."

[15] *Catalogue of Printed Music in the British Library*, vol. 33, 151.

[16] The concert took place at Covent Garden on 3 December 1844. A certain amount of controversy followed the concert because the name "Saxhorn" did not appear on the program for the concert. See Wally Horwood, *Adolphe Sax: 1814-1894–His Life and Legacy*. (Herts: Egon Publishers, Ltd., 1983), 59-60.

[17] Berlioz recalled in his memoirs: "I was engaged by Jullien, the celebrated director of the promenade concerts, to conduct the orchestra of a Grand English Opera, which he had the wild ambition of establishing at Drury Lane Theatre. Jullien, in his incontestable and uncontested character of madness, had engaged a charming orchestra, a first-rate chorus, a very fair set of singers; he had forgotten nothing but the repertory." *Memoirs of Hector Berlioz from 1803 to 1865 comprising his travels in Germany, Italy, Russia, and England* (New York: Dover Publications, Inc., 1966), 454.

[18] Carse, *Life of Jullien*, 59-61.

[19] Ibid., 71-72.

[20] George Augustus Sala, *Journey Due North; Being Notes of a Residence in Russia*. (Boston: Ticknor and Fields, 1858), 20.

[21] Carse, *Life of Jullien*, 73-74. The press offered lavish descriptions of the extravagant baton. In Boston, *Gleason's Pictorial newspaper*, proclaimed: "[It] is valued at two hundred guineas. The stick is of maple wood, and is mounted with richly-chased gold circlets, of different designs; and entwined with two gold serpents, each with a diamond in its head; next is a circlet of gold, set with seven diamonds; and the whole is surmounted with a brilliant of the value of sixty guineas; the baton is twenty-two inches in length." ("Jullien, the Artist," *Gleason's Pictorial Drawing-Room Companion*, 3 September 1853, 148.) More than a dozen years later, Tiffany produced a similar baton for presentation to the blossoming young conductor, Theodore Thomas. "The baton is made on a model of the celebrated stick used by Jullien, is mounted in 18 carat gold, and [inscribed] on a shield, surmounted by a lyre. . . Around the stick circles for half its length a broad, gold band, on which are the names of the great composers." (*Brooklyn Eagle*. 11 October 1867, 2.)

[22] Vera Brodsky Lawrence, *Strong on Music: The New York Music Scene in the Days of George Templeton Strong*, vol. 2, *Reverberations: 1850-1856*. (Chicago: The University of Chicago Press, 1995), 360.

[23] Originally constructed between 1808 and 1811 as a military fortress named Castle Clinton, the structure was roofed over in 1823, renamed Castle Garden, and began a new life as the location for popular entertainments. During its early years, with a capacity of almost 10,000, Castle Garden was the largest enclosed space in America. In September of 1850, three years before Jullien's arrival, Jenny Lind gave her first American performance in the cavernous hall. In the mid-1850s, not long after Jullien's American tour, Castle Garden again took its original name of Castle Clinton, and was converted into New York's immigration reception station. It served in that capacity until Ellis Island opened in 1892. In 1896, it was refitted again, this time as the New York Aquarium, which it remained until 1941. Today, without its roof, Castle Clinton is operated as a museum by the National Park Service and houses ticket booths for the ferries to the Statue of Liberty and Ellis Island. See Leo Polaski and Glen Williford, *New York City's Harbor Defenses*, Images of America Series (Charleston: Arcadia Publishing, 2003), 15-17 and Kenneth T. Jackson, ed. *The Encyclopedia of New York City*, ed. (New Haven: Yale University Press 1991), s.v. "Castle Clinton" by Andrew S. Dolkart.

[24] *Mirror*. 9 August; 12 August 1853. Quoted in Lawrence, *Strong on Music*, 361.

[25] *Home Journal*. 10 September 1853. Quoted in Lawrence, *Strong on Music*, 361.

[26] Ibid.

[27] *Courier and Enquirer*. 30 August 1853. Quoted in Lawrence, *Strong on Music*, 361.

[28] *Brooklyn Eagle*. 12 September 1853, 2.

[29] Ibid.

[30] *Musical Review and Choral Advocate*. October 1853, 154. Quoted in Lawrence, *Strong on Music*, 366.

[31] For a more complete discussion of Jullien's "American" pieces, see John Graziano, "Jullien and His Music for the Million" in *A Celebration of American Music: Words and Music in Honor of H. Wiley Hitchcock*, ed. Richard Crawford, R. Allen Lott, and Carol J. Oja (Ann Arbor: The University of Michigan Press, 1990), 192-215.

[32] The entire letter is printed before the music in The *Katy-did Polka, Souvenirs of Castle Garden, by Jullien*. (New York: William Hall & Son, 1853.)

[33] John Graziano ("Jullien and His *Music for the Million*," p. 214) suggests, probably correctly, that the letter from Amico may well have been written by Jullien himself as an advertising ploy. He also points out the fact that the noisemaker used to imitate the sound of the katydid, or a similar device, had been employed previously by Jullien in his 1846 piece, *The Cricket Polka*. The katydid (cricket) "equipment" was probably included in the eleven tons of baggage that Jullien transported from London.

[34] *New York Times*. 9 November 1853, 2.

[35] "The snow storm last evening prevented many visitors from attending, who would otherwise doubtless have." *New York Times*. 29 December 1853, 1. "The benefit announced last week for M. Jullien, was in a manner prevented by the very inclement state of the weather. The attendance was wretched small." *New York Times*. 30 December 1853, 1.

[36] *New York Times*. 4 January 1854, 4.

[37] Quoted in Carse, *The Life of Jullien*, 82. The letter was originally printed in the *Musical World*. 4 March 1854.

[38] *Jullien's Music for the Million* was also the title given to a collection of piano music published in New York by Samuel C. Jollie. The dedication at the beginning of the volume reads: "This collection of Popular Compositions, received with so much favor during my first visit to the United States, is respectfully dedicated to my Patrons, as a Souvenir of Their Obedient Servant, Jullien. New York, December 21st, 1853." Patterned on Jullien's Albums, which appeared annually with the New Year in London, the first copies of the book were presented as gifts to patrons of Jullien's final New York Concert, on January 3, before commencing his southern tour. "The attendance [at the concert] was unusually good, particularly in the reserved seats, where the ladies were presented with copies of M. Jullien's New Year's Album." (*New York Times*. 4 January 1854, 4.) The compilation contained a dozen pieces by Jullien, including the *American Quadrille* and other works featured on the American tour. Clearly intended to be sold at Jullien's concerts, the price was one dollar. Publisher Jollie created his own "Jullien-esque" gimmick by announcing that *Music for the Million* would be issued in an edition of 100,000 copies and that each individual who purchased a copy would be eligible to win one of the one hundred fine pianos to be given away in conjunction with the sale of the music.

[39] Broadside announcement for performance on Thursday, 11 May 1854, at the Boston Music Hall. Author's collection.

[40] "Castle Garden Last Night" *New York Times*. 30 May 1854, 4.

[41] Located at the corner of 42nd Street and Sixth Avenue, at the site of what now is Bryant Park behind the New York Public Library, the Crystal Palace was a huge cast-iron and glass building. The opening event at the Crystal Palace was America's first world's fair, called the Exhibition of the Industry of All Nations inspired by the Great Exhibition of 1851 at London's Crystal Palace. See *Encyclopedia of New York City*, s.v. "Crystal Palace" by Ivan D. Steen.

[42] The inferno was all illusion with Jullien, but four years later on 5 October 1858, the Crystal Palace did catch fire and was completely consumed, reportedly in only fifteen minutes. Ibid.

[43] The Grand Musical Congress was not the only losing enterprise for Jullien's partner, P. T. Barnum, at the Crystal Palace. Barnum accepted the presidency of the troubled Crystal Palace Company in early 1854. The venture was never successful financially. After the structure finally burned to the ground, Barnum wrote to a friend, "I was an ass for having anything to do with the Crystal Palace." (Philip B. Kunhardt, Jr., Philip B Kunhardt III, and Peter W. Kunhardt, *P. T. Barnum: America's Greatest Showman* [New York: Alfred A. Knopf, 1995], 120.)

[44] For a detailed and engaging account of Jullien's last month in New York, see Lawrence, Strong on Music, 453-471.

[45] Carse, *Life of Jullien*, 87-93.

[46] This loss probably accounts, in part, for the fact that today, aside from the published band and orchestra journals, we have none of Jullien's original music.

[47] Carse, *Life of Jullien*, 93.

[48] Carse, *Life of Jullien*, 95-97.

[49] The announcement for the Grand Musical Congress described the instrumental forces as "colossal Orchestra . . . [of] Fifteen Hundred Performers. Among them are already engaged the Germania Society, the Philharmonic Society of Philadelphia, Dodworth's Cornet Band, The United States Military Band, The Italian Opera Orchestra, M. Jullien's Full Concert Orchestra and Many Orchestral Artists and Amateurs from Boston, Philadelphia, Baltimore, Cincinnati, New Orleans, and New York." The list of choral participants included some twenty choral societies from New York, Philadelphia, Boston, and Baltimore as well as "members of the several Church Choirs" from a list of more than fifteen cities. (*New York Times*. 13 June 1854, 5.) Gilmore's prospectus announced "grand orchestra of one thousand musicians, including the leading Bands, and best performers in the United States" and a 10,000 voice chorus to include "all the Musical Societies in New England, and elsewhere available, to be united, forming the greatest Oratorio Chorus ever assembled, either in Europe or America." (*The National Peace Jubilee and Musical Reporter* [Boston], 15 May 1869, 6.)

[50] Programme. Grand Concerts. Gilmore's Band. Manhattan Beach, 18 August 1892. Author's Collection.

[51] *Brooklyn Eagle.* 11 September 1886, 3.

[52] See *Brooklyn Eagle.* 19 July 1887, 1 and 8 September 1888, 3.

[53] "Novel Features To Be Introduced at Manhattan Beach This Year," *Brooklyn Eagle.* 21 August 1889, 1.

[54] It is included, for example, on the printed program (author's collection) for a concert of the Gilmore Band at the Masonic Opera House in Oskaloosa, Iowa, on Sunday, 28 November 1886.

[55] *The Metronome.* August 1886, 5. In discussing his plan, Innes wrote, "The idea is my own though modeled on the lines laid down by Jullien."

[56] *Brooklyn Eagle.* 9 May 1880, 3.

[57] *New York Times.* 18 July 1880, 7. Another announcement (*New York Times.* 1 August 1880, 7) reported, "It is understood that Mr. Aronson has the manuscript scores of this music." Is it possible that some of Jullien's manuscripts survived the fire that destroyed his library at Covent Garden in London and made their way to America two decades later?

[58] *Brooklyn Eagle.* 8 August 1880, 3. The critics did not receive the concerts with unanimous approval. The writer for the New York Times "Metropolitan Concert Hall," *New York Times.* 5 August 1880, 5) found the old arrangements to be "decidedly thin and tame." "Listening to these commonplace jingles," he continued, "one could not but wonder that they should have ever been received with such favor as they certainly commanded in their day. However, they were received with considerable applause by Mr. Aronson's audience, and were listened to by the younger portion of the crowd with combined interest and curiosity, while their elders, doubtless, were reminded of the delights of Castle Garden a quarter of a century ago. The orchestra played the numbers in question with spirit, but even the best of orchestras could not make anything of musical interest out of this dreary old rubbish."

[59] Ibid.

New York Bands in the Nineteenth Century *by John Graziano*

The role of the band in nineteenth century America cannot be underestimated. It permeated every aspect of American musical culture, from parades to concerts both indoors and outdoors, to balls and cotillions, to opera. While orchestras were not unknown to residents of urban centers, such as New York City (where the New York Philharmonic Society gave four to six concerts a year from its founding in 1842 through the 1890s)[1], bands gave concerts of varied music almost every day. From the early years of the century, bands played music from the entire known repertory - arrangements of symphonic music and the latest operas, newly composed dance music, and marches and other popular pieces. Their role, though probably unintended for the most part, was to educate their audiences with high brow and low brow musical fare - or as described by H. Wiley Hitchcock, cultivated and vernacular. [2]

One of the most interesting aspects of the band phenomenon is the number of them playing in New York City at any one time. There is no detailed study of how many musicians might have been involved at any given time, though by estimating the number of musicians in each of the bands, one can approximate the size of the cadre. [3] For many of the announced concerts, no specific pieces are mentioned. Through a search of period newspapers, however, more specific information is beginning to be mined.

Of the many bands that performed in New York City, which, until the end of the nineteenth century, consisted solely of Manhattan, the various bands led by the Dodworth family were among the most famous. Frank Cipolla has summarized their presence in the city in his article in the *New Grove Dictionary of American Music and Musicians*. [4] In 1834, when Allen Dodworth and others split from the City Band to form the National Band, soon to be renamed Dodworth's Band, one of the chief places of employment for wind and brass players each summer were the various outdoor gardens situated in the borough. During the 1830s, Dodworth's Band was heard at Tivoli Garden, in the western part of the central city, at Charleston and Varick Streets; Dilk's Band was heard at Castle Garden, a converted fort at the Battery where many ceremonies and concerts took place; and the Boston Brass Band played at Vauxhall Garden, which was in the north eastern part of the central city, at Astor Place. A so-far-unidentified band played full concerts of overtures, opera selections, and national airs at Niblo's Garden every Tuesday and Thursday; and on the alternate evenings, they were heard during the intermissions of orchestral concerts. Tickets were twenty-five cents for the orchestra concerts, and twelve-and-one half cents for the band concerts. Even at this early date, the Boston Brass Band programmed "Gems from the Operas," and featured some of their players in virtuoso solos. [5] In 1837, they played the "Grand Finale" to an unidentified Beethoven symphony, probably the last two movements of the Fifth. [6]

The decade of the 1840s ▨

During the 1840s, a number of new bands were heard in the city; their continued presence reflects the population growth of non-English-speaking immigrants. In the summer of 1841, for example, Castle Garden was the scene of a one hour concert by Napier Lothian's Brass Band every evening at seven o'clock, while at Niblo's Garden, Rebhun's German Dance Band, consisting of eighteen instrumentalists, played galops and waltzes by Strauss (1804-1849), Lanner (1801-1843), and Labitsky (1801-1881). Another German band played at the newly renovated Apollo Musical Saloon.

The proprietor, in order to throw open his Saloons to the general public of New York . . . "has regardless of the expense, engaged . . . the highly popular German Band; Who will give a grand Instrumental and Vocal Promenade . . . The selection to consist of the most favorite Airs, Scenes, Ballads, Duetts, Trios, and Glees; also popular Overtures, Waltzes, and Galops. The doors will open at seven o'clock, at which time the German Band will perform in the Promenade Saloon until the [orchestra] concert commences at eight o'clock in the Concert Hall." [7]

In these concerts, the band not only played the popular waltzes and galops that audiences were familiar with, but also overtures to the many operas that were performed in the city. Tickets were fifty cents. Other bands heard that summer were the City Brass Band, under J. Nosher, at Vauxhall, and Dodworth's Brass Band during intermissions at the Tivoli.

In 1844, Lothian's New York Brass Band appeared at Castle Garden; their nightly fare also included opera overtures, in addition to dance music, and popular and minstrel tunes. Many of these pieces were composed or arranged by Claudio Grafulla (1810-1880), a Spaniard by birth but destined to become one of the most widely-known and respected bandmasters in nineteenth century American band history. The inclusion of minstrel tunes on these programs is interesting since the American craze for minstrelsy was just beginning. The Virginia Minstrels' New York debut had occurred only a year earlier. [8]

Hudson River cruises provided another job opportunity for band members during the hot summer months. At least two special steamship events took place during the summer of 1846. The first was a trip up the Hudson by the American Musical Institute, which hired Dodworth's band for the trip. The steamer left the city at nine in the morning and traveled "to Van Courtland's Landing," at the entrance to the Highlands, near West Point, stopping there until two in the afternoon, while the passengers promenaded and enjoyed the scenery. Then they were off to nearby Newburgh. On the way there, a fine dinner was served on the upper deck, with seating for all (limited to 100 people) at the same time, "thereby affording them an opportunity of viewing the beautiful Highlands while regaling their appetites." At four the members of the Institute sang a concert in Newburgh, and at six, they left for Poughkeepsie, where the program was repeated. The chorus members boarded the steamer for their return trip to the city at ten p.m., and after a late supper, they danced to music provided by

Dodworth's Band while cruising down the Hudson River. [9] The second event was that of the Sacred Music Society, which traveled through Long Island Sound to New Haven in August to perform Handel's *Messiah* at the Yale University commencement. They were accompanied by Lothian's Band, which provided "concerted and instrumental pieces of the first order." [10] While it is not possible to positively ascertain the size of the bands that accompanied these cruises, we can speculate that the bands probably were the same size as the band advertised a few years earlier. An 1842 program for a Sunday Sacred Concert lists the nine members (and their instruments) of Lothian's New York Brass Band–an E-flat cornetto, a cornopean, a valve trumpet, a valve bugle, a bass trombone, and tenor trombone, a tenor trumpet, and two French horns.

While bands were kept busy performing during the warm summer months, they were also in great demand at other times, especially during January and the beginning of February each year when many organizations gave cotillions or balls. In 1846, Dodworth's quadrille band numbered thirty-two players. Other bands that are found in advertisements include: a German Cotillion Band, which, depending on the engagement, could be as few as two members or as many as twenty-five, Shelton's Quadrille Band, and Lothian's Cotillion Band. Additionally, there was a German band conducted by a Mr. Munck, and the "Saxonia," conducted by a Mr. Eckhardt, which gave a concert–not well-received by the critics–of Auber's overture to *La muette di Portici*, Mendelssohn's *Midsummer Night's Dream*, and the Finale to Bellini's *I Capuletti ed i Montecchi*. [11]

The 1850s

As the population of New York City grew by leaps and bounds during the 1850s, [12] the number of bands performing matched that growth. In February 1850, for example, three brass band ensembles–Dodworth's, Shelton's, and Willis's performed at a Grand Concert and Military Festival to benefit the New York Volunteers. They joined in a grand medley of national airs that included Grafulla's *New-York Volunteers' Quick Step*. [13] In December, Dodworth's and Shelton's bands played at Tripler Hall in a theatrical benefit for the well known minstrel, Thomas "Daddy" Rice, who was in need of money. [14]

The popularity of bands in general is indicated by their presence at many important city events. At the opening ceremonies of the Crystal Palace in 1853, three bands provided the entertainment. Bloomfield's United States Band played patriotic music, and Dodworth's Band and Noll's National Guard Band played "background" music while the guests viewed the exhibits. [15] Bands were also hired to greet many famous foreign guests. When Jenny Lind arrived in New York, Dodworth's Band serenaded her to her quarters at the New-York Hotel. [16] Similarly, when Louis Jullien and his entourage arrived at the end of August 1853, Adkins's Band, under the direction of Thomas Coates, serenaded him to his hotel. [17] Two nights later, Dodworth's Band serenaded Jullien again. And when he left in the spring of 1854, he received a sendoff from yet another band. The Dodworth and Bloomfield bands also assisted Jullien in the performances of his spectacular tone poem *The Firemen's Quadrille* at the Crystal Palace, where actual fires were set in various corners of the building. [18] The arrival later that year of two of the greatest Italian singers then before the public, soprano Giulia Grisi (1811-1869) and tenor Giovanni Matteo (1810-1883), whose stage name was Mario, provided the opportunity for another welcome. Dodworth's Brass Band rather strangely, given the nature of the event, played *Giorno d'orrore!* from Rossini's *Semiramide*, the full band played the *Lucrezia Borgia Quickstep,* based on themes from the Donizetti opera, and Allen Dodworth was featured as soloist in "Casta diva" from Bellini's *Norma*. [19] This type of activity continued on a regular basis through much of the period under consideration.

In 1852, eleven bands joined to perform at a Grand Military Musical Festival. The following bands performed–Dodworth's Cornet Band, the Brooklyn Cornet Band, Shelton's American Brass Band, Adkins's Washington Brass Band, Wallace's Empire Brass Band, Wannemacher's New York Brass Band, Scheibel's National Brass Band, Fischer's Brass Band, the Troy Brass Band, the Boston Brigade Brass Band, and Noll's Seventh Regiment Band. While it is not possible to positively ascertain the size of each of the bands, if we use Camus's standard instrumentation as a guide, the ten brass bands, each with twelve players, would indicate about 120 players. Adding the Seventh Regiment Band, which probably numbered about thirty-five players; it is likely that no fewer than 150 instrumentalists participated in this concert. The program shows that for the afternoon concert, all the bands played in the opening and closing numbers, the overture to Auber's well-known opera, *Fra Diavolo* and Garner's "Kosenden" Waltz. For the evening performance, the concerted bands played at the beginning and end of each part of the concert: the *Musical Fund Quickstep* by Luigi Arditi (1822-1903), [20] a march from Meyerbeer's *Le Prophete*, the "March of the Priests" from Mendelssohn's recently published incidental music to *Athalia*, and to end the concert, Dodworth's *Grand Quickstep*. Each band gave a solo turn on each of the concerts. Their choice of repertory was current; no piece was more than thirty-five years old. It included a "Potpourri" from Verdi's recent opera, *Ernani*, which received its New World premiere in 1847, only three years after its world premiere; several operatic excerpts by Donizetti, including the Finale to act 2 of *Lucia di Lammermoor*, a scene from *Lucrezia Borgia*, and a potpourri from *La fille du régiment*; the overture to Meyerbeer's *Robert le diable*, and several pieces by leaders of a few of the bands. Scheibel, for example, programmed two of his own compositions, a *Grand Quickstep* and the *American Rifle March*; Dodworth played a *Rondo* by Max Maretzek (1821-1870); and the American Brass Band featured a *Duo for two cornets* by Grafulla.

Another event that combined bands took place in August 1858 at Jones' Woods when Shelton's and Grafulla's bands performed *The Battle of Bunker Hill* subtitled *A Military Picture Musical* by one V. Streck. The two bands, probably numbering about eighty players, advanced from the corners of the park toward no fewer than seven conductors that included Theodore Thomas, Carl Anschütz, and Maretzek, until they reached the center of the grounds. [21]

Other annual activities that kept band members working were the numerous dances that were scheduled throughout the year. Two such instances from 1855 and 1875, demonstrate the range of music played. The earlier program, for a ball in the Apollo Rooms, featured Shelton's American Brass Band, which provided the dance music. The program lists twelve quadrilles, two waltzes and schottisches followed by polkas, a medley of Spanish dances, and the required promenades. The composers whose music was heard are varied–opera composers Meyerbeer and Rossini–dance composers Labitsky, Louis Jullien, and Johann Strauss–and local composers Grafulla, Edward Loder, and D. L. Downing. During the first half, the dancers were given a rest after the eighth set, while the band offered the duet, *Giorno d'orrore!* from Rossini's *Semiramide*, and a quickstep dedicated to Captain E. A. Roberts' *Lindsay Blues*.

The 1875 program shows a few differences. While the older European composers are still represented, a number of the younger generation is also included. Thus there are pieces by Halévy, Offenbach, Wagner, Charles Lecocq, Ambroise Thomas, Victor Massé, and Michael Balfe. Josef Gung'l (1809-1889), who had toured the United States in 1848-49, has joined the dance composers, and rather surprising, a Promenade from Verdi's *Aida* was included as the second half of number three, only a year after its New York premiere.

One ball of great significance occurred during the Civil War. On 5 November 1863, Gothamites entertained Russian officials just a few days after Election Day. Though the country was in the midst of the darkest days of the War, New York officials literally laid out the red carpet for Admiral Lisovsky and the Captains of his fleet. The *New York Times* (5 November 1863) said the event would make all prior balls that had taken place in the city "pale." The Academy of Music and Irving Hall were connected by a covered gallery. The two halls were decorated over a two day period, after the performance of Maretzek's opera troupe ended at midnight on 3 November. The Russians were clearly impressed, and, according to the *Times*, exclaimed "None but Americans could accomplish such a feat!" The interior of the Academy was divided into several areas: there was a private apartment for the Russians "elegantly draped with American and Russian colors." Hanging over the cloakroom was a "canopy of richly-colored silk and muslin," decorated with the Imperial Russian eagle, and lace curtains hung from the windows in the passageway. All the corridors were newly carpeted in crimson, and there were lithograph portraits of the royal family. Among the other items in the corridors were photographs of the Russian Admiral, his staff, and American Admirals, including Farragut, by the American photographer Matthew Brady. Many other pictures, including one of Czar Nicholas, also were on view. The main corridor "was lined with bronze and plaster statues representing fauns and graces," as well as a marble bust of Washington and a sculpture by Emma Stebbins (1815-1882).

The parquet of the Academy was converted into a dance floor that measured 150 by 52 feet. The stage was turned into a tent; above which was "a finely-executed painting on canvas . . . 52 feet long, 30 feet deep; represents the Genesis of America–a beautiful Indian girl in her native costume, clasping hands with the Genesis of Russia–a female clothed in furs. The figures are reclining, and above and between them is the figure of Peace, bearing the olive branch, the whole surmounted by the Russian shield; between the two female figures is the coat-of-arms of the City of New York." The artist was Minard Lewis (1812-?), who specialized in panoramas and landscapes. In front of the main entrance to the ballroom (the theater) the decorators hung an eight foot facsimile of the Russian man-o'-war Grand Admiral which was built by Americans for the Russian government to use in the Crimean War, but was never delivered because the British government objected on the grounds that it would be a breach of neutrality. After the ball, the model was to be sent to Russia as a gift for the Czar.

Irving Hall, where the guests would dine after the dancing, was likewise decorated. The main room was 100 feet long and 71 feet wide and had tables on three sides with seating for up to 800 people. The food was catered by New York's premiere restauranteur: "DELMONICO will, for the first time, have here a fair and open field, and intends to make the occasion his battle of the Pyramids–(no allusion to the creams and jellies)–his Austerlitz. At the Prince of Wales' Supper, he was pinched for room . . . but here the whole basement . . . will be at his disposal, and he can make an effort worthy of his 'genius'." The guests arrived for a reception at 9 p.m.; at 10 o'clock they departed for the ballroom, where the Russian men were introduced to their American dancing partners–"the great pride of New-York, its charming daughters." The dancing began at 10:30 and continued for an hour. At 11:30, the assembled guests took the covered passage to Irving Hall for the banquet, at which food would be served "until the festivities are closed." The American planning committee hired two fifty-piece bands to play at the Academy. Forty men played during the banquet; it is not clear whether they are some of the same men who played for the dancing.

The bands chosen by the floor committee were Grafulla's and Helmsmuller's. The former played the promenade and operatic music, while the latter provided the music for the dancing. The bands were located on opposite sides of the auditorium, in the second tier. The *Times* published the dance program on the morning of the ball. Grafulla's Seventh Regiment band opened with the overture to Rossini's *William Tell* and selections from *Ernani* (probably the same arrangement that was used in 1852), and ended with a performance of Russian and American National Airs. Helmsmuller's Seventy-First Regiment Band then began the dance music, which consisted of twenty-one sets. Most of the pieces were arrangements of operatic arias and instrumental pieces, though there were several original waltzes, polkas, and galops by Helmsmuller, Grafulla, Emanuele Muzio (1825-1890), Strauss, and Gung'l. The arrangements drew on numbers from Rossini *(Semiramide)*, Meyerbeer *(Dinorah, L'etoile du Nord,* and *Robert le Diable)*, Verdi *(I due Foscari, Nabucco, Un ballo in maschera, Il trovatore, Macbeth, Attila, and La traviata)*, Donizetti *(Poliuto, La fille du régiment, Don Pasquale, and Linda di Chamounix)*, Flotow *(Martha)*, Offenbach *(Orphée aux Enfers)*, Errico Petrella *(Ione)*, and William Balfe *(The Enchantress)*. Of the forty-two pieces heard at the ball, at least twenty can be identified as operatic excerpts, proving how popular these pieces were with the public. Especially interesting is the inclusion of the excerpt from Petrella's opera, which had not yet received its American premiere. In this case, the band was introducing new music to its listeners and if later they attended the opera, those tunes would be regarded as familiar "old friends." Of the remaining pieces, two were especially composed for the event: Helmsmuller's *L'alliance Joyeuse* galop, and Grafulla's *Flag of the Free* march. The music performed at the banquet is not specified.

Only one other city paper covered the event. Contrary to the glowing report in the next day's *Times*, the *Post* was far less positive about the ball. After commenting on the unexpected warm temperature that left people uncomfortable, the reporter noted that:

> When Helmsmuller's excellent orchestra [sic] struck up the music for the dance, frantic efforts were made to clear a sufficient space for the dancers, but such was the pressure of the swaying and heaving crowd that it was nearly impossible to place the sets in position, and when the task had finally been accomplished the amusement became hard labor. There was imminent danger of irreparable injury to elaborate toilettes and peril to ribs; but for all this the dance went on in a crowded fashion, and [as] the heat intensified itself the dancers gave up in despair and fled to the lobbies and boxes in search of air. [22]

The *Post* also commented on the banquet: "we noticed that the ladies sometimes came off second best, on account of the remarkable preponderance of the male sex. A double file of men, many of them unaccompanied, for a time barred access to the tables, and the unusual spectacle of ladies waiting while men ate was visible in more than one corner of the room." [23] Yet this ball was clearly the outstanding social event of the year. Throngs of people stood outside the Academy to see the rich and famous enter the theater and there was one advertisement in the *Times* that offered three tickets at a scalper's prices of $25 each.

Outdoor concerts were heard throughout the summer and into the fall in the city. Bands could be heard in the various gardens, such as Niblo's, or in the city's parks, including several places in Central Park, or in a number of private parks, such as Jones's Woods, which occupied an area bounded between Sixty-Sixth Street and Seventieth Street from the East River to Third Avenue; today, part of the woods is occupied by New York Hospital. Many concerts are listed and sometimes reviewed in the newspapers.

During the 1860s, advertisements and announcements gave notice to the numerous band concerts taking place all over the city. [24] After the defeat of the Confederate States, the extent of the celebration on July 4 gave an early indication of the expansion of musical activities in the city. On 4 July 1865, for example, the Municipal Authorities of the city placed an advertisement in the *New York Times*:

"The Joint Committee . . . has the honor to submit the following:

> There will be a military parade of the First Division N.Y.N.G. under command of Major-Gen. Charles W. Sandford. . . . In the evening, fireworks will be exhibited at the following places and in order of the programme. . . . During the interval between the pieces, aerial fireworks will be displayed in rapid succession, and the bands will furnish music at the following places, viz.:City Hall–Grafulla's Band., East Broadway and Grand-st.–Hill's Band, Madison-square–Grafulla's Band, Tompkins-square–Robertson's Band, West Broadway and Franklin-st.–Robertson's Band, Broadway and 43d-st.–Kingsland's Band, Jackson-square–Kingsland's Band, Battery–Rubell's Band, Union Market-square, East Houston-st.–Kissenberth's Band, West Houston-st.-square–Kissenberth's Band, Marion and Spring sts.–Manahan's Band, Monroe and Market-sts. Mount Morris-square–Rubell's Band, 64th-st., between 8th and 9th avs.–Blind Band, Liberty-square–Kingsland's Band, 8th-av. Park–Kingsland's Band....At the City Hall there will be a fine display of fireworks set off. At the other places above designated there will be a similar display."

During the afternoon at 3:30, Harvey Dodworth and his band gave a concert on the Central Park Mall, which, in addition to the usual operatic excerpts, included Downing's quickstep, *Welcome Home*.

On 6 July, the *Times* reported on the Union Square parade, saying it was somewhat different from the published program: More than 7,000 men marched, not counting those in the twelve bands that accompanied them around the square. Undoubtedly, band members were busy throughout the day as well as during the evening fireworks displays.

The musical explosion was not limited to band performances. Many more orchestra concerts were offered as well. Theodore Thomas formed a full time orchestra that played many concerts in and around the city. Between 1866 and 1868, Thomas offered a summer series of popular concerts in Central Park. In order to entice a large audience, Thomas offered a subscription to the entire season–100 concerts–at ten cents each. For ten dollars, one could listen to a concert of symphonic music every night from the middle of June through the middle of October! An examination of Thomas's programs for his summer concerts demonstrates the strategy of his approach–play the same mix of music that people heard at band concerts. I have reproduced the programs of two band concerts and one orchestral concert on pages 41 and 42 that took place during the second half of 1866. The first is a Thomas concert from August at the Terrace Garden in Central Park, which was intended to introduce New York audiences to cultivated music. As was the case with band concerts, his programs were a mixture of opera overtures and potpourris, symphony movements, and lighter pieces that included polkas, marches, waltzes, and other dances. On his 11 August concert, Thomas programmed some operatic excerpts–the overtures to Auber's 1841 opera, *Les diamants de la couronne*, Rossini's *Semiramide*, and Flotow's *Martha*; a selection from Petrella's *Ione* (1858), which had received its New York premiere the previous season, and the already famous quartet from Verdi's *Rigoletto*. Although Auber's opera was twenty-five years old, it was still being performed in the city from time to time; audiences would have been very familiar with the overture. Rossini's *Semiramide* was no longer part of the standard repertory, though it had received two performances during the previous season. Its overture and several other numbers were heard regularly and appear to have been audience favorites. Flotow's *Martha*, premiered in 1847, was well-known in the German community; Anschütz had presented it with his German opera company during the 1862-63 season. Thomas's choice of a selection from Petrella's *Ione* [*Jone*] and the already famous quartet from Verdi's *Rigoletto* reflect the current popular taste in 1866. *Ione* had recently been produced by Maretzek; while the critics were mostly lukewarm to the opera, the public's curiosity about an opera that chronicled the last days of Pompeii kept it in the repertory for twenty-four performances over three seasons. While it was not as popular as *La traviata* or *Il trovatore*, by 1866, *Rigoletto* was a staple of the repertory, and the quartet would have been known by virtually the entire audience. Thomas also included a potpourri of lighter pieces by Gung'l, Lumbye, and Strauss, among others. Dodworth's band concert, a week earlier, also included several overtures–Rossini's *Il Barbieri de Seviglia*, and Wallace's *Lurline*; a "grand selection" from Verdi's *Attila*, (which had not been successful when it was heard in New York in 1850), and a march by the Ricci brothers from their comic opera *Crispino e la comare* (1850), which had recently been premiered by Maretzek's troupe; lighter music by Strauss; and a variety of pieces by local composers–Allen or Harvey Dodworth, Thomas Baker, and Coote. The concert of 18 August by the Central Park Band is similar in content with two overtures, dance music, and several operatic selections. Outdoor concerts continued into the fall. Dodworth's Band appeared on the Central Park Mall in late October, and most surprisingly, on 18 and 26 December at the Fifth Avenue Skating Rink, where they serenaded skaters just south of Central Park.

During the 1870s, band repertory continued to reflect changes in the musical scene. Programs combined the music that was heard during the previous decades with newer pieces. For example, in May 1870, a band concert in Central Park performed a selection from Verdi's seldom-heard 1844 opera, *I due Foscari*. While it was not in the repertory, several bands continued to play some of its arias and ensembles that by the 1870s were familiar to their audiences. Also heard was the Overture to *Guillaume Tell*, a work that still survives today on "pops" concerts. Newer works included Offenbach's overture to *Orphée aux Enfers*, which was being performed regularly as part of the *opéra bouffe* "invasion" that all but eclipsed other operas during the late 1860s, and von Suppé's overture to *Die Frau Meisterin* (1868). A concert later that year contrasted music from Bellini' *La sonnambula* (1831) and Auber's *Le cheval de bronze* (1835) with Offenbach's *La Grande-Duchesse de Gérolstein* (1867).

There are a number of questions that are still unanswered. How many band musicians were active in New York during the middle of the nineteenth century? In

1860, Harvey Dodworth's "full" band was advertised to be sixty men. Were they the same men who played in smaller Dodworth ensembles? At one Fourth of July celebration, no fewer than three Dodworth bands were playing in various parts of the city. An article from that year tells us that Noll's Seventh Regiment Band and Shelton's were merged to form a band of forty. Yet in another article, it is stated that the Seventh Regiment band was thirty-five strong. And there were at least another ten to twelve bands in the city during this period. If each of them were twenty or twenty-five players strong, there would have been about three hundred active wind and brass players in the city. Some also may have played in the bands heard in Brooklyn (then a separate city), but undoubtedly there were additional musicians living and working there as well.

Another question is how many of these men played in the theater orchestras, of which there were at least five during the 1860s and 70s, or whether those jobs generally went to the instrumentalists of the New York Philharmonic and Theodore Thomas orchestras? Lists of players have not yet been discovered. In general, band musicians appear to have been fully employed. As is the case with today's freelancers, the better-paying jobs probably were offered to the more reliable players; the Dodworth enterprises appear to have functioned as a band and booking venue through much of this period, which would account for their being able to place men in several locations at one time.

In spite of the cooperative nature of the engagements, including mammoth festivals and holiday celebrations in which competing bands joined to play, there is evidence of some competition among them. In January 1866, a notice appeared in the New York press that Dodworth's Twenty-Second Regiment Armory Band would be playing concerts nearly every Saturday evening. The concert on February 3 includes selections from Wagner's *Tannhauser* and Donizetti's *Don Sebastian*. On the same day, the papers announced that the Seventh Regiment Band, conducted by Grafulla, would offer concerts "nearly every Saturday evening" as well. No program is given for the concert of February 3, but I think we can surmise from these advertisements that Grafulla was not going to let the Dodworths continue their dynasty unopposed. Much is yet to be written on the importance of band concerts to the dissemination of contemporary music in the mid-nineteenth century. As my research continues, I am sure many new items of importance will surface and I will be able to document the vitality and strong presence that made bands the primary conveyors of popular musical culture for the public during much of the nineteenth century.

Concert of August 11, 1866
by the Theodore Thomas Orchestra,
Central Park Garden

Piefke: "Doeppel" March

Rossini: Overture to *Semiramide*

Johann Strauss, Jr.: "Promotionen" waltz, op. 221

Petrella: selections from *Ione*

Flotow: Overture to *Martha*

Heindl: "Carnival of Venice" with solo flute

Gung'l: "Paulinen" Polka

Lumbye: "Traumbildern" fantasie

Auber: Overture to *Crown Diamonds*

Verdi: Quartet from *Rigoletto*

Bach: Grand potpourri

Central Park Band
4 August 1866

Dodworth: "Aquatic" March

Rossini: Overture to *Il barbieri di Siviglia*

Baker: "Three Guardsmen" waltz

Golde: Adagio and Rondo

Johann Strauss, Jr.: "Leopoldstädter" polka, op. 168

Wallace: Overture to *Lurline*

Coote: "Songs of Olden Time" quadrille

Ricci: March from *Crispino e la comare*

Dodworth: "Green Hill" notturno

Berckhardt: "May" polka

Kuhner: "Forward" galop

Central Park Band
18 August 1866

Johann Strauss, Jr.: "The Attack" March

Auber: Overture to *Le chaperon blanc*

Moore: "Tis the last rose of summer"

Cooke: "Passion-flower" waltz

Komsak: "Robin" polka

Kucken: Overture to *Die Flucht nach der Schweiz*

Jullien: Caledonian" quadrille

Gluck: Grand selection from *Iphigenia in Tauris*

Friesing: "The Belle" quickstep

Dodworth: "The Shamrock Garland"

Doppler: "Ohne Rast und ohne Ruh" galop

Boston Brass Band, Eben Flagg, Leader

Brass bandsmen with over-the-shoulder brass instruments and contrasting regimental uniforms.

Handbill for Dodworth's Musical Festival, February 20, 1853.

Notice the appearance of Master [Theodore] Thomas as violin soloist and the introductory performance of Mendelssohn's *Grand Military Overture* as performed by Dodworth's "Full Band."

Handbill for Grand Military Musical Festival at Castle Garden, September 4, 1852 featuring eleven brass bands.

Harvey B. Dodworth (1821–1891) with an A-flat over-the-shoulder brass instrument.
Painting by Charles Waldo Jenkins.

NOTES

[1] Henry Edward Krehmiel, *The Philharmonic Society of New York: A Memorial* (New York and London: Novello, Ewer and Co., 1892), Appendix.

[2] H. Wiley Hitchcock, *Music in the United States: a historical introduction,* 4th ed. (Upper Saddle River, N.J.:Prentice Hall, 2000), 37.

[3] In his article in the *New Grove Dictionary of American Music and Musicians* (1:128), Raoul Camus gives totals for specific bands from 1781 to 1983. For 1854 and 1861, he lists a representative instrumentations of twelve- and seventeen-piece brass bands, respectively.

[4] Frank Cipolla, s.v. "Dodworth," in *The New Grove Dictionary of American Music,* ed. H. Wiley Hitchcock and Stanley Sadie (London" Macmillan, 1984), 1:639–40.

[5] Vera Brodsky Lawrence, *Strong on Music: Resonances 1836–1850* (New York: Oxford University Press, 1988), 34.

[6] Lawrence, *Resonances,* 43.

[7] *New York Herald,* 17 September 1841.

[8] Lawrence, *Resonances,* 283.

[9] Ibid., 399–400.

[10] Ibid.

[11] Ibid., 549.

[12] The population of the city was 515,394 in 1850, 629,810 in 1855, and 814,254 in 1860, according to *Manual of the Corporation of the City of New York* by D. T. Valentine (New York: Edmund Jones & Col, 1866), 414.

[13] *New York Herald,* 2 February 150.

[14] Vera Brodsky Lawrence, *Strong on Music: Reverberations 1850–1856* (Chicago: The University of Chicago Press, 1995), 116.

[15] Lawrence, *Reverberations,* 345.

[16] Ibid., 44.

[17] *Spirit of the Times,* 13 August 1853.

[18] Lawrence, *Reverberations,* 469.

[19] *The Musical World and Times,* 26 August 1854.

[20] Arditi was resident in New York between 1851 and 1858; he conducted various opera troupes and had his opera, *La spia,* produced at the Academy of Music in 1856.

[21] Vera Brodsky Lawrence, *Strong on Music; Repercussions 1857–1862* (Chicago: University of Chicago Press, 1999), 187.

[22] *The New York Post,* 6 November 1863.

[23] Ibid.

[24] The *Music in Gotham* project, of which I am co-director, is attempting to trace every musical event that took place in New York City (i.e., Manhattan) between 1862 and 1876. To construct this chronology, we are searching through every extant New York City newspaper and periodical for advertisements, articles, and reviews.

Turn of the 20th Century

James Reese Europe and African-American Bandleaders of the World War I Era *by Tim Brooks*

I wonder how many people know the name of the first major recording "star"? Or, the name of the first ensemble that would have won a gold record, if they'd had them at the dawn of the record industry?

First of all, it would have been a gold cylinder, because that's what records looked like then. The "superstar group," believe it or not, was none other than the United States Marine Band. Those musicians were probably the best selling celebrity artists on record in the 1890s.

Band music was, in fact, one of the most popular forms of recorded music during the first quarter century of the record industry, from 1890 to the mid 1910s. Other best selling bands on record included those of John Philip Sousa (after he left the U.S. Marine Band), Arthur Pryor, Walter B. Rogers, Patrick Conway, Charles A. Prince, and Patrick Gilmore. Gilmore's musicians continued to record under his name even after he was dead!

America was very segregated then, and most record buyers were white. Racial discrimination, sometimes referred to as "the color line," was deeply embedded in American law and custom. However, a number of black artists did record, as described in my book, *Lost Sounds: Blacks and the Birth of the Recording Industry, 1890-1919.* [1] The first black band to record in the U.S. played dance music, a very syncopated style, a kind of precursor to jazz. Its leader was a tall, commanding figure by the name of James Reese Europe, and his life is a remarkable story. [2]

James Reese Europe

Europe was born in Alabama in 1880 and raised in Washington, D.C., in a middle class black family. His father worked for the postal service under Republican administrations. In 1899 his father died suddenly, and the family's finances became strained. In 1902 Jim Europe joined his brother John in New York City where the two brothers tried to carve out careers in music. A gregarious sort, Jim hung out at the Marshall Hotel on West 53rd Street, a gathering spot for black musicians, and soon became known in the black music community. He had his setbacks, but over the next decade he slowly built a solid career writing and conducting for black musicals, which were then enjoying a vogue in Northeast cities.

Europe had a more ambitious goal in mind however - to improve the lot of black musicians in the New York area. They were excluded from the white unions, and worked for minimum wages under the worst possible conditions. There had been several attempts to address this situation, but without much success. In 1910, Europe and some of his friends formed the Clef Club, a combination social club, booking agency and union for black musicians. He plunged into its work with enthusiasm, setting up a clubhouse and insisting on high standards of musicianship and professionalism among the members. He was a natural leader, and found no lack of followers.

To draw attention to the Club, he promoted a series of Clef Club Concerts. These were held twice a year in large venues and were elaborate affairs featuring a one hundred-piece orchestra including ten pianos and scores of mandolins and related string instruments. The repertoire emphasized a type of rhythmic, syncopated music that was very progressive for the time. Job offers came pouring in.

In 1913, Europe himself was engaged by superstar white dancers Vernon and Irene Castle to be their "hot" bandleader (they also had a white "sweet" band for waltzes). Europe's association with the Castles, who were then at the height of their fame, brought him to the attention of a much wider audience. In December 1913 he was invited to record for the Victor Talking Machine Company, the largest record company in America, under the Castles' auspices. These were the first commercial recordings made by a black orchestra in the United States. Recordings were still being made acoustically at this time (no microphones, just a big horn connected to a mechanical recording device). According to the recording ledgers, the instruments in front of the recording horn were five banjo mandolins, three violins, one clarinet, one cornet, one trap drum and one piano ("two playing it").

The repertoire was varied, but included up-tempo numbers such as *Too Much Mustard* and *Down Home Rag*. *Too Much Mustard* was given a fast, loose and limber performance, with shouts from the band members, cymbal crashes and frantic drumming by the energetic Buddy Gilmore. Edgar Campbell's clarinet took the lead, with Gilmore's drumming prominently behind him, a most unusual arrangement for the period. The high energy, four minute rendition must have been exhausting to dance to. *Down Home Rag* by black bandleader Wilbur Sweatman, was played even faster. Violins and drums predominated, egged on by encouraging shouts from the musicians. At times the drums faded out, leaving the fast-sawing violins to go solo, lending an even more varied sound. At the end the whole ensemble played a fast "shave and a haircut, two bits" figure, as if to exclaim "that's all, folks!" It sounded like a party in progress. The strait-laced Victor studios had seldom seen anything like this.

It is interesting to compare these performances with those of standard white bands, generally all brass that recorded the same selections at about the same time. The Columbia version of *Too Much Mustard* was by Prince's Band, which played it at a similarly fast tempo, but in strict military time, with cornet and trombone predominating and blocks used for rhythm. The drums are not even audible, and the overall effect is stiff and mechanical. The same selection had been recorded about a year earlier by the Victor Military Band under Walter B. Rogers, again with traditional military instrumentation, and with brass taking the lead and a tuba for rhythm. There were no shouts from the musicians. Europe's striking recordings were best sellers.

During the following years Europe led an active life performing with the Castles, writing, touring and serving as unofficial leader of New York's black musicians (first in the Clef Club, and later in another organization called the Tempo Club). In May 1916, he was approached by Colonel William Hayward, the commander of the 15th New York National Guard Infantry Regiment. The 15th was an all-black regiment under white officers, and it was having trouble with recruiting during the nervous days when America was trying to stay out of the war that had erupted on the other side of the Atlantic.

Hayward wanted Jim Europe to take over the regimental band and play at recruiting drives, in order to help spur enlistments. Europe was patriotic, but he also had very high musical standards, and a period of negotiation followed in which Hayward sought sponsors to fund the first-class military band that Europe envisioned. Finally he succeeded and Europe took the assignment, accepting a commission as a lieutenant (rare for a black American then). And what a band he put together! First he persuaded some of the best players in New York to fill the ranks, then when he couldn't find enough good reed players locally, he went to Puerto Rico to recruit some there. He also put together an adventurous repertoire for the time, including ragtime and other "hot" music. Enlistments soared.

By December 1917, the United States was at war and the Regiment, now renumbered the 369th Infantry, sailed for France. Europe's instrumentation was military, but it was a swinging band, and it is widely credited with having introduced jazz to France. The French fell in love with "le jazz hot," a love affair that has continued to the present day.

Every commander wanted Europe's band to play for his troops, and the band ended up performing all over the continent. Jim Europe insisted on personally serving for periods of time on the front lines as well, in a machine gun company, and became an authentic war hero. The entire regiment distinguished itself in battle, fighting so fiercely that it was dubbed "The Hell Fighters." Europe's now-famous band became "The 369th U.S. Infantry 'Hell Fighters' Band."

The Regiment returned to New York in early 1919 and Europe's Band—90 men strong—led a huge parade up Fifth Avenue, playing hotter and hotter as they approached Harlem. The city went wild. Soon after that, Europe set about organizing a tour of the Northeast, and most of his men agreed to stay with him for the tour. Their concerts would include a wide variety of music, popular and standard, hot and sweet, played by the band and augmented by a troupe of individual vocalists and vocal groups.

As the band was about to leave, they were engaged by the Pathé record company, resulting in a marathon series of recording sessions during March and May, 1919. In all, twenty-eight titles were released, reflecting the wide variety of music being featured on the tour. About half the selections were Tin Pan Alley pop tunes, but the rest were an interesting mixture of blues, rags, spirituals and specialty numbers that accompanied production sequences in the concerts.

The band is perhaps shown to best advantage in the blues and rags. While not as uninhibited as in the wild 1913 Victor recordings (no shouts from the band), it is an extraordinarily loose aggregation, exuding enthusiasm and good cheer. There are jazzy riffs, buzz cornets, hot clarinets and even an occasional "shave-and-a-haircut" stinger. No military band had ever sounded like this on record!

Among the best of the popular tunes was the rousing end-of-war hit, *How Ya Gonna Keep 'Em Down on the Farm (After They've Seen Paree)?* Many bands and vocalists had recorded this smash hit, but none with such drive and enthusiasm as Europe's musicians—who had, after all, lived the song's lyrics? Cornets and trombones alternated with flutes in a fast, vaudeville-style opening, followed by a clever bridge, and then a vocal chorus by Noble Sissle, who almost shouted the words in a style reminiscent of Eddie Cantor (who was featuring the song in vaudeville at the time). By the time Sissle was finishing, the band was really cooking; barely able to be restrained, it came charging in on top of the end of his vocal, never losing momentum as the song built to an exhilarating conclusion. One wonders if Europe simply signaled the band to "go for it" during the last thirty seconds or so. This recording contrasts sharply with the carefully planned and executed arrangements heard on most records of the period. It was also a unique sound for a military band, pointing the way toward swing bands of later years. [3]

The day following its last recording session Europe's troupe appeared in Boston, after which it was scheduled to move on to a big final concert of the tour in New York City. But during the Boston performance, on May 9, 1919, Europe was suddenly and unexpectedly attacked backstage by a mentally unbalanced young musician named Herbert Wright, whom the fatherly band leader had taken under his wing and had been trying to help. Wright inflicted a stab wound that was at first thought not to be life threatening, but Europe suffered severe loss of blood. He died later that evening in a Boston hospital.

Reaction to Europe's death was overwhelming. There was a huge turnout for his funeral in New York, reportedly the first ever public funeral for an African-American in the city's history. Thousands filed past his casket. He was buried at Arlington National Military Cemetery.

James Reese Europe had ambitious plans, for more tours, for all-black musical shows, and for a National Negro Symphony Orchestra. He hoped to take the exciting music of African-Americans to a whole new level, and many were ready to take that journey with him. We will never know what this charismatic leader might have accomplished during the "Jazz Age" of the 1920s. As it is, he is remembered as a true pioneer, both for what he did for black musicians and for laying the groundwork for what would eventually become big band jazz.

Another African-American band leader of the World War I era, and a close associate of James Reese Europe, was a talented musician named Ford Dabney. Little has been written about Dabney, but he was a highly influential black musician in the early 1900s, and he made many recordings - although they are devilishly hard to find today.

Dabney was born in Washington, D.C., in 1883 to a musical family. Both his father and uncle were professional musicians, and the latter, Wendell P. Dabney (1865-1952), went on to achieve considerable renown as a music educator and author. Young Ford received musical instruction on the piano and, by the age of twenty, was ready to begin his own career in music. In 1904, after a few theatrical engagements, he accepted a job that must have sounded like a real adventure for a young man - that of court musician to the President of Haiti. Haiti was an extremely poor and violent country, but it was black-ruled, and thus idealized by many African-Americans. During Dabney's three years there, the country was in constant turmoil, and shortly after he returned to the U.S. in 1907, his patron, the President, was overthrown and run out of the country.

Dabney then embarked on a career conducting and composing for the black theater, shuttling between Washington and New York. He composed several successful songs, including *Oh You Devil*, *The Haytian Rag* (in honor of his recent adventure in that Caribbean nation) and *Anoma*. Another composition was only moderately successful at the time, but would eventually become his greatest hit: *That is Why They Call Me Shine*.

Dabney struck up a friendship with the rising young conductor Jim Europe and, in 1910, joined him in founding the Clef Club. He and Europe became quite close professionally, with Dabney serving as principal pianist in, and co-leader of, Europe's orchestra. He played piano on Europe's historic 1913-1914 recordings for Victor, and one of the selections recorded then *(Castle Walk)* was co-written by Dabney and Europe. In fact, the pair collaborated on numerous dance tunes for the Castles, becoming virtual "house composers" for the famous dancers. Legend has it that they provided the music for one of the most popular dances of the twentieth century, the fox-trot, a dance invented by the Castles.

In addition to his work with Europe, Ford Dabney appeared with his own orchestra from time to time, although these were essentially pick-up bands as opposed to a regular organization. In June 1914, he was hired by Broadway mogul Florenz Ziegfeld to provide the music for his new after-theatre dance club called the "Danse de Follies," in the roof garden room of the New Amsterdam Theatre, which was open following the main Ziegfeld Follies show. The club was so successful that it evolved into a combination dance club and late night vaudeville performance called Ziegfeld's Midnight Frolic, featuring many of the Follies stars in a more intimate setting. Originally, Dabney was supposed to play for only part of the show, alternating with a white orchestra, but Ziegfeld liked the energy and syncopation of the black musicians so much he eventually gave them the job exclusively.

The Midnight Frolic, high above Broadway, became one of the trendiest shows in town for New York's elite, and Dabney's syncopated orchestra became the toast of high society. He was renewed year after year and, by 1917, was one of the best known bandleaders in the city. In the spring of that year, the revolutionary sounds of jazz filled the air, sparked by the first recordings of the Original Dixieland Jass Band, and record companies were scrambling to find performers who could play the new music. Dabney was approached by the Aeolian-Vocalion company, a maker of high quality phonographs and musical instruments, which had just begun stockpiling recordings in anticipation of a label launch in early 1918.

Dabney's first recordings, made in mid 1917, were a mix of Tin Pan Alley pop tunes and syncopated novelty songs, some by black composers, mirroring the kind of music he was playing for the trendy dancers at the Midnight Frolic. It wasn't really jazz, but rather was played in a relatively strict tempo for dancing, albeit with a certain looseness and verve characteristic of the new music. The heavy use of cornets and piccolos, and rat-tat-tat drumming, makes these early sides sound a little like a somewhat raggy military band.

Perhaps recognizing Dabney's talents as a bandmaster, Vocalion had him record several straightforward marches with a real military band in 1918 and 1919, some billed as by *Dabney's Military Band*. *Our Sammies March*, *A Winning Fight* and *Mr. Sousa's Yankee Band* were spirited affairs with cornets blaring, piccolos twittering, cymbals crashing and drums pounding in march tempo. The stirring performances were perfect for the patriotic times and, while not as innovative as the recordings of Jim Europe, hold their own with those of any white military band of the time. [4]

Dabney remained with Ziegfeld until 1922, and then became a full-time composer and publisher. In 1923 he revived one of his early songs, shortening the title to *Shine*, and saw it become one of the biggest hits of 1924. It went on to become a jazz standard, recorded hundreds of times in the decades that followed. A million-selling version in 1948 by an energetic newcomer named Frankie Laine introduced the song to a later generation. Dabney lived a long life, and passed away in New York in 1958, his story largely untold.

Other African-American Bandleaders of World War I ⬚

Several other black bandleaders of the era played with the same loose, enthusiastic jazz-infused feeling as Jim Europe, although they did not record at the time.

Will Vodery (1885-1951) was a songwriter, show conductor and arranger for Florenz Ziegfeld for twenty years beginning in the early 1910s. During the war, he led the 807th Infantry Regiment Band across Europe, playing in a style similar to that of James Reese Europe. Later he became a mentor to numerous young black musicians, including Duke Ellington. In the 1920s and beyond, he worked on Broadway shows and later Fox motion pictures, becoming the studio's first regular black arranger.

Tim Brymn (1881-1946) also began his career conducting and writing for black musicals, including those of the famous comedy team Bert Williams and George Walker. During the war, he led the 350th Field Artillery Regiment Band, another of the organizations credited with "introducing jazz to France." In the 1920s, he led a jazz band called the Red Devils, which recorded for the Okeh label.

Egbert E. Thompson (? -1927), born in Sierra Leone, was active in the Clef Club and Tempo Club and was Jim Europe's predecessor as leader of the 15th Regiment Band. He remained active in the Regiment and was another of the 369th Infantry's bandmasters during the war. He settled in Europe after the war where he led a number of dance bands. He is not known to have recorded. [5]

Summary ⊠

The African-American bandleaders of World War I have a number of things in common.

First, they brought their own unique "voice" and repertoire to band music. Military bands, such as those of Sousa, had experimented with ragtime and other forms of syncopation before, but improvisation was largely antithetical to band music. The black bands brought a looseness and enthusiasm that was new to American listeners, certainly on record, presaging jazz. These bands also spread the music of black ragtime and jazz composers.

During the war years, the black bands brought jazz to Europe, which fell in love with it. They also introduced the new music to thousands of American soldiers, who brought it home with them, helping fuel the Jazz Age of the 1920s.

The black bands provided a training ground for many jazz musicians of the 1920s and beyond. Leaders like Vodery and Brymn went on to significant work in the theater and on film. In many ways the army bands of the war years showed black musicians they could find an international audience for their music, as played by their own ensembles. Some of these musicians relocated to Europe after the war and had long careers there.

At least two of these African-American band pioneers recorded, leaving us an important legacy. Unfortunately, due to sweeping and highly restrictive copyright laws passed in the U.S. in recent decades, reissues of recordings from this period are not readily available to Americans today.

Finally, the influence of James Reese Europe in organizing African-American musicians and sparking this movement cannot be overstated. He was a mentor to many, and a guiding light to black musicians in the dark, racist years leading up to the 1920s. His innovative arrangements lay the groundwork for what would become big band jazz, but more than that, he was a war hero and a personal symbol.

As Eubie Blake put it years later, "People don't realize yet today what we lost when we lost Jim Europe. He was the savior of Negro musicians. He was in a class with Booker T. Washington and Martin Luther King. I met all three of them. Before Europe, Negro musicians were just like wandering minstrels. Play in a saloon and pass the hat and that's it. Before Jim, they weren't even supposed to be human beings. Jim Europe changed all that. He made a profession for us out of music. All of that we owe to Jim. If only people would realize it." [6]

James Reese Europe

Europe and his jazz band

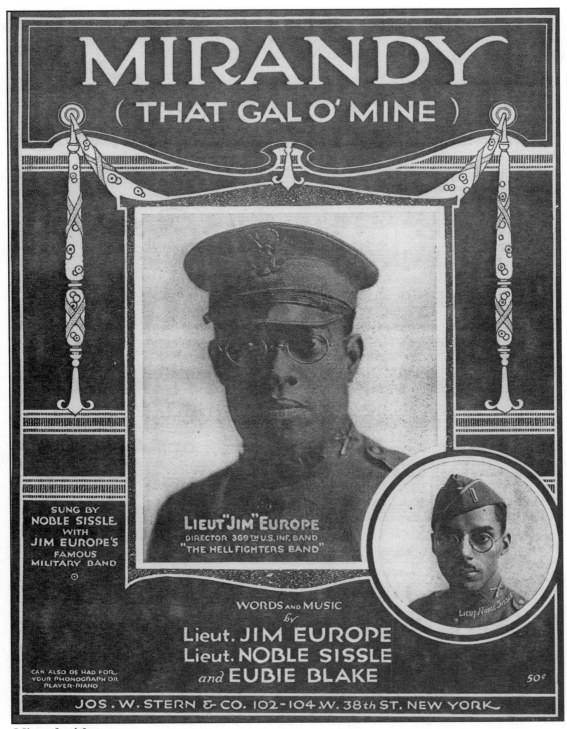

Mirandy title cover

On Patrol in No Man's Land **sheet music**

On Patrol In No Man's Land
Pathé Fréres phono label

Pathé Records advertisement

St. Louis Blues **Pathé Records phono label**

Europe and the 369th in an outdoor performance

Pathé Records advertisement

Ford T. Dabney

NOTES

[1] Tim Brooks, *Lost Sounds: Blacks and the Birth of the Recording Industry, 1890–1919* (Urbana, IL: University of Illinois Press, 2004).

[2] The standard biography of Europe is Reid Badger, *A Life in Ragtime: A Biography of James Reese Europe* (New York: Oxford University Press, 1995).

[3] Two CDs were released in 1996 each containing the complete Pathé recordings by the band. They are "Lieut. Jim Europe's 369th U.S. Infantry 'Hell Fighters' Band: The Complete Recordings," Memphis Archives MA7020; and "James Reese Europe Featuring Noble Sissle: The Complete Pathé Recordings,: IAJRC CD-1012, the latter produced by the International Association of Jazz Record Collectors. There is no single collection of the 1913–1914 Victor recordings; a few individual titles have appeared on compilations, as listed in *Lost Sounds,* 583. None of the Victors have been reissued by the copyright holder, Sony BMG Music.

[4] Few of Dabney's recordings have been reissued. A small discography of reissues can be found in *Lost Sounds,* 585.

[5] Short biographies of Vodery, Brymm and Thompson can be found in Eileen Southern, *Biographical Dictionary of Afro-American and African Musicians* (Westport, CT: Greenwood Press, 1982).

[6] Al Rose, *Eubie Blake* (New York: Schirmer Books, 1979), 60–61.

Charles Ives's Manhattan *by Jonathan Elkus*

One of Charles Ives's twice-told tales was about the time his father George helped a drunken Stephen Foster home following his collapse on a New York sidewalk. This was during the immediately pre-Civil War winter of 1860-61, when George was in the city studying harmony, counterpoint, and cornet, and attending the Philharmonic Society's four seasonal orchestral concerts. Edith Wharton recalls that era's monotony of "the old Fifth Avenue with its double line of low brown-stone houses, of a desperate uniformity of style …"[1] In fact, "desperate uniformity of style" could describe the Danbury, Connecticut, of George's birth and growing up, as well as the musical models and etudes that he had gone to New York to study from his German-born tutors. Forty years later, it was the young Charles's turn to live in New York, as he would for the rest of his life. He was in his mid-twenties, right out of Yale, and devoted to music, athletics, and conviviality. He was to become an urbane New Yorker whose memory of simpler days and music making in Danbury would merge with the complex reality of his adopted city and find expression in a far-reaching expansion of musical language.

Charles was no stranger to New York's abundance. While in New Haven prepping for Yale at Hopkins Grammar School, he had taken the train one Saturday morning to attend a matinee of *Die Götterdämmerung*. Through the noontime crowds and in warm, sunny weather he walked "immediately to the Theater in time to get a good seat in the family circle," the top gallery of the Metropolitan Opera House's recently electrified Golden Horseshoe.[2] Walter Damrosch conducted a cast headed by Amalie Materna and Anton Schott. Busoni was in town, and Barnum & Bailey's "Greatest Show on Earth" was playing at the Garden on Madison Square. Farther uptown, in Carnegie's splendid Romanesque-revival Music Hall, Damrosch conducted his New York Symphony *("increased to 73 musicians") that Sunday evening in "Tchaikovsky's great Symphonie Pathétique."*[3] Back in New Haven the following Tuesday, a buoyed-up Ives pitched a 10–9 victory for the Hopkins nine over the Yale freshmen.

By the time Ives moved to New York in 1898, the city itself had become a veritable stage set, thanks to the centralization of Civil War profits and resourceful architectural eclectics like Richard Morris Hunt and Stanford White, whose mansions, clubs, and high-end shops like Tiffany's now adorned Fifth Avenue. (Alas, many fewer of these remain today.) Much of Manhattan was burrowed by massive engineering projects. Electrification made possible the underground main lines and yards for the new Grand Central and Pennsylvania Stations, as well as for the inter-borough subway systems; electrification replaced steam locomotion on the deafening elevated railways - the Els ("Ls" as Ives spelled it) - while on the streets, the clangor and grinding of electric trolleys drowned out the still-purposeful clatter of horseshoes and rumbling of iron-rimmed wheels. Tracks and overhead wiring went everywhere. And, with the advent of the Bessemer steel process, substantial older buildings were dwarfed within months by soaring skyscrapers.

Among musical New Yorkers, enthusiasm for the expanding tonal dimensions of Debussy and Strauss was fast eclipsing the appeal of Wagner; but, for everyone else, ragtime was the thing - and for Ives, too. Writing in 1915, the critic and essayist James Huneker summed it up:

> New York has been called a calamity, a freight yard, a boiler-shop, an open trench, a mining gulch - with its manners and tastes; in reality it is the most aggressively noisy city on earth. ... She may be enormously vulgar, and the genius of her is enormous, and never suggests mediocrity. You may hate or love her, but you cannot pass her by; and if Stendahl were alive today, he would rechristen the city Cosmopolis, the noisiest cosmopolis that ever existed, but also the New Cosmopolis, the most versatile city on our globe.[4]

Ragtime certainly contributed to the city's racket. Competing pianists from the open doors and windows of neighboring taverns, apartments, and music shops greatly extended the tonal and rhythmic complexities with which George Ives had experimented back in Danbury during Charles's growing up; but in the New Cosmopolis there arose an accompaniment of urban clatter that applied a constant, but ever-varying, cantus firmus to the ragtime. In Ives's mind, the cacophony of rivet guns and steam shovels could even have taken on a musical life of their own.

Ives settled in for the summer of 1898 at the old Yale Club, on Madison Square North. Lining the two visible streets of the adjacent northeastern block were the inviting Venetian colonnades of Stanford White's Madison Square Garden, that fabled sports and entertainment complex, whose search-lit tower was crowned by Saint Gaudens's huge copper weathervane, a sleek, naked representation of Diana the Huntress. Madison Square was considered not merely the center of town but - in O. Henry's words - "The Center of the Universe."[5] Ives's first workplace was in an office of the Mutual Life Insurance Company, in their imposing building bound by Nassau, Liberty, and Cedar Streets. (The successive locations of the Ives and Myrick agency were never to be far from these corners.) On Saturdays, work ended at noon so there might be time for a more leisurely lunch at one of the downtown restaurant-taverns where Ives would become a regular over the next thirty years. Then perhaps, a walk in Battery Park with his co-worker and future business partner, Julian ("Mike") Myrick, and a ballgame pitched for one of the company's teams - later, for his agency's team. From Battery Park, downtowners could see daily the great transatlantic liners sailing in or out with the tides. These floating hotels (as they were called), each recognizable by its profile and frequency, were as familiar as the sight of any prominent building. Spotting a liner would be like greeting or saying "so long" to a friend on the street.

For the next ten years, Ives shared quarters with different bachelor friends, many from Yale, among whom was David Twichell, Ives's future brother-in-law. Though the location changed several times, all these quarters were in Midtown and all were called "Poverty Flat."[6] The dwelling the group held the longest was on Central Park West—

that is, Eighth Avenue - facing the ten-acre ball ground still in the southwest corner of the Park. The Eighth Avenue trolley passing their building took followers of the National League Giants uptown to the Polo Grounds.[7] The Ninth Avenue El took Ives downtown to work. Some six blocks to the north stood the Dakota Flats, a forbidding block of luxury apartments (so named in irony because the developer's rivals had scoffed at the elegant complex being built "way up there in Dakota Territory" - that flat, rural northerly stretch west of Central Park being the closest Ives ever got to the Great Plains of his cowboy namesake *Charlie Rutlage*). From the Dakota's rooftop could originally be seen - beyond and to the right of Poverty Flat itself - the steeple of Central Presbyterian Church on West Fifty-seventh Street, two blocks west of Carnegie Hall, where Ives was organist and choirmaster for two years and where the 1902 premiere of his cantata *The Celestial Country* marked the end of his nearly fifteen years as a professional church musician.[8]

Two of Ives's surviving church pieces that represent the original works he played at Central Presbyterian, and which have been transcribed for modern wind band, are *The Collection* (included in the Elkus-made suite *Old Home Days*) and *Postlude in F.* These reflect the then-fashionable French manner of Saint-Saëns and Massenet, with their sensuously placed chromatic passing tones.[9] A third and more venturesome church piece (though, like the *Postlude*, from his New Haven days) is his *Fugue in C*, where the voices answer in G, D, and A, along the circle of fifths.

But, Ives's floodwater of new expression following his emancipation from the time, energy, and artistic constraints any church job demands was like a dam breaking. One after the other, even simultaneously, he produced studies and sketches for piano, small ensemble, and theater orchestra that reflect not only an astonishing musical sophistication, but also the urbanity of a confirmed New Yorker. Besides Manhattan's omnipresent concert of noise, Ives had assimilated at least a sampling of new music from Europe, including Mahler, Scriabin, and Sibelius (in addition to Debussy and Strauss), going well beyond their rhythmic and tonal boundaries. In some of these studies and sketches, he set up a scheme of rhythmic and/or tonal regularity, against which superimpositions proceed with independent commentary. Of these studies, *Central Park in the Dark*, *Over the Pavements*, *Three Ragtime Dances*, *The Unanswered Question*, and *Yale-Princeton Football Game* are perhaps the most famous.[10] But to wind band people, two particular works from Ives's Poverty Flat decade stand out: *"Country Band" March* and *Overture and March "1776."* The first is a raucous travesty, fashioned by our tavern-wise Charlie - that super-achieving city kid - to show his country cousins how they don't play ragtime (or anything) right, and to point out how naïve they are to think that throwing out familiar phrases from square old songs could even remotely pass for improvisation. The second–*"1776"*–is, however, every bit the theater piece that Ives intended it to be. Its beginning - an eerie dream-frame of bugle calls, an implied patriotic song, and off-beat drum patter - is summarily dispelled by the parallel major triads of a pit band's attention-getting "Let's go!" fanfare that ushers in the march and trio and its melee of horseplay - Ivesian "band stuff" that features the mixed-up cornet shanks. The return of the dream-frame heads us this time into wild bugle-call flourishes and an explosive "Curtain up!" tag. As Huneker says, "aggressively noisy."[11]

Ives's Manhattan included the theater district, then concentrated around Fourteenth Street. There he found copyists, whom he was able to engage with increasing frequency and theater orchestras, that he could hire in the late hours to read through his music. Sometime in 1907, at the beginning of his courtship of Harmony Twichell, he began the extensive sketches toward his *Second Symphony*, which was to be completed in 1910. This symphony is not only a patriotic musical tribute to his own father and to Harmony's - both were Civil War veterans - but also a nuptial offering to Harmony and her family. The symphony testifies to Ives's uncommon ability as a composer and, as a man of character, affirms his Christianity (the Twichells were devout) and his tenacity and his optimism. Similarly, Schumann had composed his *First Symphony ("Spring")* for his pianist fiancée - and no less her pianist father - in testimony to his skill in the "larger forms" (as multi-movement works were called to distinguish them from most salon music). Except for the Finale's final three-measure tag - which Ives appended considerably later - the *Second Symphony* includes none of the far-reaching musical experiments that marked his Poverty Flat years. Rather, it is a substantial, mainstream work, grandly planned (like Bruckner's) and painstakingly worked out from overtures and organ music that Ives had written years before.[12] And partly because it is based on colloquial melody (patriotic songs, hymn tunes, Stephen Foster) and partly because it derives from popular orchestral works that even in 1907 had already had their day (like Dvořák's *"New World" Symphony* and Chadwick's *Jubilee*), it is a winsome work, to use Swafford's adjective, one in which everyone might find familiar bearings. For Ives the artist the *Second Symphony* is a nostalgic, backward look; for Ives the forward-looking downtowner, it was to prove his ace in the hole.

The Iveses lived in middle-class comfort in a succession of apartments and town houses, and tried suburban living in Hartsdale for a few years. The rail commuting agreed with Ives, giving him solitary time away from family, business, and the piano to draft his literary, political, and business essays, the prefaces and post faces to his musical works, and training programs for his agents. Only on the train, and secluded in his downtown office, could music freely mix with business: the one helped the other, Ives said. The commutes lengthened when the couple built a cottage in West Redding, Connecticut, where they typically spent the warmer half of each year, Ives commuting to the new Grand Central Terminal and then via the Third Avenue El to his office.

These are the years of Ives's completion and self-publication of his *Second Piano Sonata* - the *"Concord,"* intensive work on his symphony *Four New England Holidays*, and his worked-over gathering and self-publication of *114 Songs*.[13] Among the Manhattan-related songs in the *114* are *Ann Street* (downtown, near Ives's office), *The Cage* (Central Park Zoo), *Two Little Flowers* (the Iveses' backyard, 120 East Twenty-second Street), and *Waltz* (Bowery, in *Old Home Days*). From the *"Concord"* come three transcriptions for wind band of its third movement, *"The Alcotts"*;[14] from the *114 Songs* come transcriptions of *The Circus Band* (with additions from a still later source) and *A Son of a Gambolier*, which in Ives's revision for the *114* becomes the most contrapuntally sophisticated of his Yale-period marches; from the *Holidays* symphony comes a transcription of its second movement, *Decoration Day*, one of Ives's superb memorializations of his boyhood, his father and the Civil War, his father's Danbury Band, and "band stuff." But although a hometown musical occasion again draws the Manhattanite "from the city,"[15] the substance and manner of *Decoration Day's* musical expression stay in New York.

Certainly Ives's greatest cityscape is a work that he himself considered among his finest and one that became the third movement, *Hanover Square North*, of his *Second Orchestral Set*.[16] The prompting of that movement by a traumatic event illustrates Ives's absorption in (and of) his surroundings. On the morning of Friday, 7 May 1915, the nation was stunned by the news that the British liner *Lusitania* had been torpedoed off the coast of Ireland without warning and with a huge loss of life. For the better part of a decade the *Lusitania* had been a bi-weekly visitor to New York harbor, and many New Yorkers had sailed on her. The shock felt throughout the United States must have been like the shock felt on Pearl Harbor Sunday and September 11, 2001. Ives's account of the day clearly reveals his sensitivity to the prevailing mood:

> I remember, going downtown to business, the people on the streets and on the elevated train had something in their faces that was not the usual something. Everybody who came into the office, whether they talked about the disaster or not, showed a realization of seriously experiencing something. (That it meant war is what the faces said, if the tongues didn't.) Leaving the office and going uptown about six o'clock, I took the Third Avenue "L" at Hanover Square Station. As I came on the platform, there was quite a crowd there waiting for the trains, which had been blocked lower down, and while waiting there, a hand-organ or hurdy-gurdy was playing in the street below. Some workmen sitting on the side of the tracks began to whistle the tune, and others began to sing or hum the refrain. A workman with a shovel over his shoulder came on the platform and joined in the chorus, and the next man, a Wall Street banker with white spats and a cane, joined in it, and finally it seemed to me that everybody was singing this tune, and they didn't seem to be singing in fun, but as a natural outlet for what their feelings had been going through all day long. There was a feeling of dignity all through this. The hand-organ man seemed to sense this and wheeled the organ nearer the platform and kept it up fortissimo (and the chorus sounded out as if every man in New York must be joining in it). Then the first train came in and everybody crowded in, and the song gradually died out, but the effect on the crowd still showed. Almost nobody talked— the people acted as though they might be coming out of a church service. In going uptown, occasionally little groups would start singing

or humming the tune.

Now what was that tune? It wasn't a Broadway hit, it wasn't a musical comedy air, it wasn't a waltz tune or a dance tune or an opera tune or a classical tune, or a tune that all of them probably knew. It was only the refrain of an old Gospel Hymn that had stirred many people of past generations. It was nothing but *In the Sweet Bye and Bye*. It wasn't a tune written to be sold, or written by a professor of music - but by a man who was but giving out an experience.

Like his descriptions of communal singing at the rural camp meetings of his youth, this account shows yet again how deeply Ives was moved by the ability of ordinary music to express the shared emotion of ordinary people. In a breaking wave of released tension, *Hanover Square North* affirms such interrelatedness between social and musical values. As Ives goes on to explain:

This third movement … comes from that "L" station … and its general make-up would reflect the sense of many people living, working, and occasionally going through the same deep experience, together. It would give the ever changing multitudinous feeling of life that one senses in the city.[17]

In 1926, Charles and Harmony, their daughter Edith, and Ives's resident whipping boy, Rollo (an Ives-invented character who personified the genteel music critics whom he had come to detest), moved into their final family residence, a brownstone at 164 East Seventy-fourth Street. It was opposite the Mannes School of Music [18] and a half block from the Third Avenue El, Ives's route to work until he retired in 1930. His music room was in the attic, on the fifth level. There, after both health and composition failed him, he puttered among his manuscripts, revising and annotating and improvising on them at the piano. People had begun to inquire about him and his music, and his often expansive replies were dictated to Harmony and Edith. He dictated his Memos and recorded acetate discs of his piano improvisations at a midtown studio. He made plans with Henry Cowell, Lehman Engel, Lou Harrison, Bernard Herrmann, John Kirkpatrick, and Nicholas Slonimsky and others about performance and publication, which - typically - he subsidized. He brought Milhaud home to lunch one day after a rehearsal. The Myricks and the Ruggleses were always welcome; family from both sides was often with them. All the while he continued to encourage the making of the legendary rural Ives: the rugged New Englander, the "Connecticut Yankee" of music, the musical Currier and Ives - the maverick, the loner. Even in declining health, his abiding patriotism inspired a World War II update of one of his World War I songs, now expanded for chorus and orchestra and re-named *They Are There! (A War Song March)*; it too is transcribed for modern wind band.[19]

John Kirkpatrick premiered the *"Concord"* at Town Hall, New York, in 1939. As a result of its success - as evidenced particularly by Lawrence Gilman's review ("the greatest music composed by an American") - Ives's Class of '98 invited Kirkpatrick to play *"Concord"* for them at the Yale Club (now on Vanderbilt Avenue, across from

Grand Central). One of Ives's classmates told Kirkpatrick afterward that it was "just like hearing Charlie play."[20]

Henry and Sidney Cowell were on hand to write the first life-and-works biography of Ives. Despite his habitual and ever-louder disdain for the genteel, Ives could hardly ignore that an orchestral performance in Carnegie Hall would ipso facto confer a seal of approval from the Rollos of the musical world. The Cowells' biography points to Ives's ambivalence about public acceptance:

> Ives always said that if his *Second Symphony* were ever performed in Carnegie Hall, he would go to hear it, for it was full of nostalgic references to music of the period when his father was still alive, and he thought he could enjoy listening to it. To have his music played in the great concert hall that was associated with his early concert-going in New York, when he must have dreamed that music of his yet to be written would one day be heard there, was obviously something he had hoped for in his lifetime.[21]

Leonard Bernstein premiered the *Second Symphony* with the New York Philharmonic in Carnegie Hall on the night of Washington's Birthday, 1951. The performance was a triumphal success. Mrs. Ives and family and the Cowells were there; the ailing Ives had been taken to West Redding to stay with neighbors, on whose radio some ten days later he heard the broadcast of a subsequent performance.

Ives died in the May of 1954 in Roosevelt Hospital at Ninth Avenue and West Fifty-ninth Street. His manuscripts and photostat negatives were sorted by John Kirkpatrick and others at Edith's apartment on East Fifty-seventh. Before delivering these materials to the Yale Music Library on Mrs. Ives's behalf, Mrs. Cowell assembled a complete set of positive prints for the New York Public Library, whose music collection now resides at its Library for the Performing Arts at Lincoln Center. In 1955 wreckers began demolishing the Third Avenue El, ushering in a new era of sunshine and serenity along its "long, noisy, blighted, nostalgic" route.[22] Following Bernstein's death in 1990, his heirs brought his library of performance scores from the conductor's final New York residence, the Dakota Flats, to the New York Philharmonic Archive at Lincoln Center.[23] Among them was the score of the *Second Symphony*. Thus, both the whole of Ives's life work in music and his first Carnegie Hall triumph rest archivally across the street from the site of the hospital where he died and a block west of the ball ground in Central Park.

This article is expanded from my extemporized talk subtitled "Saturday Ball and Carnegie Hall," the opening presentation of the thirty-second national meeting of the College Band Directors National Association, held at the Park Central Hotel, New York City, on February 24, 2005. The focus of the gathering explains why the compositions of Ives's whose contents I discuss are those with which wind band conductors are likely to be especially familiar; to hear these works, the reader is referred to the United States Marine Band CD-17 (*Symphonies of Wind Instruments,* 2001) and CD-19 (*Charles Ives's America,* 2003). The acknowledged facts and generally accepted viewpoints concerning Ives's life and work are to be found in one or more of these standard works: Henry Cowell and Sidney Cowell, *Charles Ives and His Music* (New York: Oxford [1955], 2nd edition, paper, 1969); Vivian Perlis, *Charles Ives Remembered: An Oral History* (New Haven: Yale, 1974 and since); James B. Sinclair, *A Descriptive Catalogue of the Music of Charles Ives* (New Haven: Yale, 1999); and Jan Swafford's biographical study *Charles Ives: A Life with Music* (New York: Norton, 1996). Actual quotations from these sources and others are cited individually. Although my New York talk was illustrated with original picture postcards circulated among the audience, the illustrations here, unless otherwise credited, are from *King's Handbook of New York City* (Boston: King, 2nd edition, 1893). To better see Ives's New York through his own eyes, I refer the reader to these Dover publications: *Thirty-two Picture Postcards of Old New York* (ed. Cirker, 1976); Mary Black, *Old New York in Early Photographs,* 1853–1901 (2nd edition, 1976); and Andreas Feininger and John von Hartz, *New York in the Forties* (1978). Philip J. Lowry's *Green Cathedrals* (Cooperstown: Society for American Baseball Research, 1986) features vintage photographs of the Eighth Avenue Polo Grounds and the nearby ballparks of Ives's time. Timothy A. Johnson's *Baseball and the Music of Charles Ives: A Proving Ground* (Lanham, Md.: Scarecrow Press, 2004), likewise well illustrated, draws parallels between Ives's musical development and the rise of baseball as the national pastime. Charles Lockwood's *Bricks and Brownstone: The New York Row House 1783–1929* (New York: Rizzoli, 2nd edition, 2003) includes photographs of row house developments in a variety of New York City neighborhoods and districts. A chronological list of Ives's addresses is included in Sinclair, 722–23. I am grateful to Diana King, Suzanne Eggleston Lovejoy, Rachel Marshall, and Ben Walsh for research, and to Sondra Reid for guidance in preparing this article.

Grand Central Railroad Station, East Forty-second Street and Vanderbilt Avenue, around 1892. Note horse-drawn streetcars in foreground.

Madison Square Gardens (1890–1925), southwest corner around 1892.

A southbound steam-powered Third Avenue El train approaches Coenties Slip from Hanover Square, around 1892. In the background is the East River, looking toward Brooklyn.

Mutual Life Insurance Company of New York, Nassau and Cedar Streets, around 1892.

Central Presbyterian Church, 220 West Fifty-seventh Street, around 1892. Ives was organist and choirmaster here, 1900–1902.

East Seventy-fourth Street, the Iveses' final New York residence.

Photograph by Kathy Sobb, 2005.
Reproduced by permission

NOTES

[1] Edith Wharton, *A Backward Glance* (New York: Appleton-Century, 1936), 1. The sense of the entire passage is glossed effectively by Edwin T. Rice in *Musical Memories* (New York: privately printed, 1943): "After a sojourn abroad in her early childhood, Mrs. Wharton returned to New York in the seventies, and records her horror at the monotony of the city's streets, and the entire absence of architectural distinction and charm in its appearance" (9).

[2] From Ives's letter to his father in Ives, *Essays Before a Sonata and Other Writings,* Howard Boatwright, ed. (New York: Norton, 1961 and since), 250, n41.

[3] Quotations and specific information from advertisements (headed "Amusements"), Daily Tribune (New York: April 29, 1894), 11. According to Damrosch's advertisement, Ives's seat in the Family Circle cost one dollar. And Damrosch, like Ives himself, kept a frenetic schedule, alternating his Saturday afternoon *Götterdämmerung* and Sunday evening *Pathétique* with Mendelssohn's Saint Paul on Friday afternoon and Saturday evening. A photograph of Ives in his Hopkins uniform may be found in Cowell and Cowell, Johnson, Perlis, and Swafford.

[4] New Cosmopolis: *A Book of Images* (New York, Scribner, 1915), 72 and 148. Compare Henry James: "Henrietta Stackpole was struck by the fact that ancient Rome had been paved a good deal like New York, and even found an analogy between the deep chariot- ruts traceable in the antique streets and the over-jangled iron grooves which express the intensity of American life." *The Portrait of a Lady* (New York: Random House [Modern Library], 1966; first published 1881), 286.

[5] From Andy Logan, *That Was New York: The Palace of Delight*, The New Yorker (27 July 1965), 41.

[6] The name "Poverty Flat" - presumably a pun on Bret Harte's famous title - belied the size and service amenities of these quarters.

[7] Presumption of Ives's attending big league baseball around New York rests only on his three musical sketches of ballplayers, discussed in Johnson, chapters five and six.

[8] Photograph (1887) from the Dakota rooftop, Lockwood, 248. The Dakota still stands, nestled now among the high-rises facing the Park. Central Presbyterian is long demolished (and with it a substantial quantity of Ives's original musical material that he'd left in the library).

9 In 1893, Ives had attended a recital by Guilmant, the forerunner of the French organ school, at the World's Columbian Exhibition in Chicago.

[10] A precursor to these studies is Ives's boyhood burlesque of *London Bridge*, adapted in *Old Home Days*.

[11] Ives combines *Country Band* and *1776* in *Putnam's Camp,* the central movement of his *First Orchestral Set (Three Places in New England)*. But in framing both pieces as a young boy's dream (which he narrates in a superscription), Ives repudiates the immediacy of *Country Band* and dulls the zest of its reality. (*Country Band* is Ives's equivalent of Mozart's *Ein musikalische Spaß* - properly called "A Musical Jest," though actually more a parody of kapellmeister composition than of the playing by the village musicians themselves.) The Verdian microcosm of *1776*, mm. 1-16, is Ford's *È sogno o realità?* in *Falstaff* (New York: Broude Bros., n.d., 189). For more on "band stuff" see J. Elkus, *Charles Ives and the American Band Tradition: A Centennial Tribute* (Exeter, UK: The American Arts Documentation Centre, 1974), 22ff.

[12] The fourth and fifth movements of the Second Symphony are, together, a "slow-fast" overture (as are the first and second movements). They are recorded as a pair on the U.S. Marine Band CD-17.

[13] All of Ives's songs are now printed in the single volume *129 Songs*, H. Wiley Hitchcock, ed. (Middleton, Wisc.: A-R Editions, Inc, 2004), RRAM XLVII and MUSA XII.

[14] The transcriptions are by Richard E. Thurston (1968, for the U.S. Tactical Air Command Band), Maurice Gardner (1969 [published as Concord Village]), and J. Elkus (1998, for the U.S. Marine Band).

[15] *Go, my songs! Draw Daphnis from the city* is Ives's paraphrase of Virgil that begins the song *Old Home Day* (whose chorus is in *Old Home Days*).

[16] The movement's full title is *From Hanover Square North, At the End of a Tragic Day, the Voice of the People Again Arose.*

[17] *Ives, Memos,* John Kirkpatrick, ed. (New York: Norton, 1972), 92–93.

[18] The Ives house still stands; the former Mannes School is demolished.

[19] Ives's 1943 acetate recording (piano and voice) is reproduced on the CD *Ives Plays Ives* (New York: CRI, 1999), 38–40.

[20] Conversation with John Kirkpatrick, New Haven, around 1975.

[21] Cowell and Cowell, 135.

[22] *New York Times* (31 July 1955), 60; (29 April 1973), 24.

[23] Telephone conversation with Richard Wandel, New York Philharmonic Archive, March 1996.

Duke Ellington and Percy Grainger: Black, Brown, and "Blue-Eyed English" *by Laura Rexroth*

October 25, 1932 marks the little-known meeting of two unlikely-matched musical masters. Duke Ellington and his orchestra performed for a class taught by Percy Grainger at New York University. How did this meeting come about? What was Grainger's interest in jazz? Why did Ellington consent to this kind of "instructional" performance at this point in his career? What do these two seemingly disparate artists have in common?

According to John Hasse, Ellington's manager Irving Mills was probably responsible for the performance at NYU.[1] Mills worked hard to gain credibility for Ellington in musical circles outside of jazz, especially pushing the image of Ellington as a "legitimate" composer.[2] Mercer Ellington seems to confirm this when he comments on Grainger's comparison of Ellington to Bach and Delius: "This, and similar observations made in Europe that year encouraged Irving in his efforts to elevate the stature of the orchestra and to urge increasing veneers of sophistication on the music."[3] This kind of lecture-performance in the classroom of a highly regarded classical performer/composer would have been a way of increasing Ellington's credibility. [It is interesting that a full concert for the college was not arranged to reach a larger number of students.] All of this conjecture makes sense. But although there is no hard evidence to suggest it, Grainger may also have extended a personal invitation. At the very least, it appears he would have been very happy to accept such a proposal from the Ellington camp.

Grainger first encountered jazz (mostly in the form of ragtime) in London music halls around 1902. One of his piano pupils from this period remembers that he used to improvise at the piano in a similar rhythmic style.[4] He was also very attracted to the instruments used in the orchestra pit in these music halls, particularly the "tuneful percussion" instruments. (Grainger would retain this love of mallet and pitched percussion sounds for the rest of his life and feature these instruments prominently in his compositions.)

During the period 1903-09, Grainger composed a virtuosic dance piece for piano entitled *In Dahomey* that embraced material from minstrel shows and early jazz styles. Wilfred Mellers described it as:

> Grainger's quintessential piece of piano virtuosity, 'a wonderfully jazzy romp (as John Pickard puts it in his liner notes to Jones' CD performance), which would surely have established instant popularity were it not so horrendously difficult to play'. Grainger subtitled it 'Cakewalk Smasher', and smash it does, in the style of the dance fantasias of the early nineteenth-century New Orleans piano virtuoso Louis-Moreau Gottschalk, who was an even more outrageous showman than Grainger. . . Grainger's piece swashbuckles in rip-roaring fiesta, adrift in what eighteenth-century Dr. Burney called 'extravagant and

licentious modulations', and as riotously abandoned as a New Orleans honky-tonk pianist, note-clusters, double glissandos, warts and all. A performer today—even a Martin Jones—can hardly avoid a generous sprinkle of wrong notes, and these wrong notes are right.[5]

As early as 1924, Grainger was an advocate of the new jazz music. His article in the September issue of *The Etude* reflects an intellectual and musical interest in jazz that is entirely opposite opinions stated in the previous month's "Jazz Problem" issue by such luminaries as John Philip Sousa and Walter Damrosch. He writes about the musical characteristics of jazz as extensions of classical music-categorizing it as "the finest popular music known to me in any country of today or even of the past. . . There never was a popular music so *classical*."[6] Grainger's article must be read with a filter for both the racial stereotyping of the day and Grainger's own tremendously odd (and oftentimes disturbing) philosophies. In spite of this, he does list several "achievements" of jazz, such as its instrumentation (he felt it "opened up glorious instrumental possibilities"),[7] the use of the saxophone (a favorite instrument of Grainger's), the use of percussion to add clarity, the introduction of vibrato (he felt all wind instruments should be played with vibrato, similar to accepted string vibrato), and the "noticeable impression" jazz had made on the works of modern German composers (observed when he visited Europe the summer before).

Grainger further defends this music:

> Seductive, exotic, desocializing elements imputed to Jazz by musical ignoramuses have no musical basis. Musically speaking, the chief characteristics of Jazz are solidity, robustness, refinement, sentiment, friendly warmth. As music it seems to me far less sensuous, passionate or abandoned than the music of many peoples.[8]

Grainger enjoyed the music of jazz musicians such as Duke Ellington, Paul Whiteman, and Ben Pollack. He included their music in his "musical melting pot", claiming in a letter to D.C. Parker:

> All styles and types of music find a positive response in [my] musical nature and there is not one that [I] would exclude from [my] world of music. . . I am the only composer known to me who loves every kind of music (of whatever locality and period) that he has ever heard . . . be it classical or jazz, art-music or folk-music, highbrow or lowbrow, medieval, polyphonic, romantic, atonal, futuristic or what-not.[9]

Grainger was apparently familiar with current literature on jazz as well. To prepare his students for Ellington's visit, he led a discussion of R.D. Darrell's *Black Beauty*—the first critical article on Ellington's music published in *disques* magazine in June, 1932.[10] He quoted extensively from sections linking Ellington's music with that of Frederick Delius. Grainger agreed with Darrell's pairing and felt that 'Ellington's music had a harmonic language similar to Delius'.[11] Even if Grainger had not respected Ellington's music before, this comparison would have encouraged a closer connection, as Delius was an admired colleague and friend.[12] On the day of Ellington's visit, Grainger introduced the bandleader to an overflowing classroom: "The three greatest composers who ever lived are Bach, Delius and Duke Ellington. Unfortunately Bach is dead, Delius is very ill, but we are happy to have with us today, The Duke."[13]

To further prepare his students, Grainger lectured on the "high emotional and technical qualities in Ellington's music—rapturous moods, sustained melodiousness, imitation of the human voice by instruments, polyphonic texture, and rhapsodic improvisation by individual players of the orchestra."[14] To illustrate his points, he compared a recording of Delius' *The Walk to the Paradise Garden* with Ellington's *Creole Love Call* and *Creole Rhapsody*.

The Walk to the Paradise Garden was added to the score of Delius' most successful opera, *A Village Romeo and Juliet*, five years after it was completed in 1901. The plot of the opera is a dark, romantic tale of doomed young love. Beginning with simple, spun-out melodies, *Paradise Garden* has several small climaxes where the melodic material receives more urgent treatment—faster rhythmic patterns and the use of chromaticism. The themes are constantly treated to changes of color, using the different wind, brass and string choirs. The final sweeping climax relaxes in a long decrescendo and thinning of texture until a calm, softly sustained ending. Although the comparison does seem unusual, all of Grainger's "high emotional and technical qualities" identified in the music of Ellington can be heard in this piece by Delius (especially if the sinuous, somewhat wandering rhythms of the melodic line are interpreted in the Debussy-ish manor of "rhapsodic improvisation").

Although Grainger's comparison to Delius was reportedly confusing to Ellington (and probably to many others), it was most likely Delius' harmonic language that reminded him the most of Ellington's music. The following description is just as true of Ellington as it is of Delius:

> The strength of Delius' personality is most evident in a harmonic style which sounds quite unlike the work of any other. . .The [chordal] syntax is entirely individual. The rate of harmonic change is extremely flexible, sometimes so fast as to border on atonality, at other times hypnotically slow. The more chromatic harmonies can wind sinuously downward, or they may be abruptly juxtaposed. . .it is the irregular ebb and flow of the harmony that is the prime structural factor, belying the melodic simplicity. Indeed Delius' melodies are rarely complex and usually seem to be stitched into the texture merely to point the harmony.[15]

Although Grainger's lectures were not well attended (students quickly grew tired of his oftentimes outrageous statements), his lecture with Ellington was full to overflowing. He initiated a discussion of Ellington's music, posing questions such as: "Art music is defined as music fixed by notation—to what extent is Ellington's music art music (fixed by notation), to what extent does it admit free improvisation (varying with each performance) by individual players?"[16] Grainger declared the balance of tone in a jazz band (3 clarinets, 3 trumpets, 3 saxophones, rhythm section) was more perfect than the finest symphony orchestras. He summarized the components of Ellington's jazz as combinations of "various elements of 'classical' music: Polyphony, chamber music, refinement of tone, display music (virtuosity) as in Chopin and Liszt, rapturous mood (as in Delius), and pre-Bach music."[17] Grainger considered the "gliding and off-pitch sounds in jazz" an important step toward the Free Music of the future.[18]

Grainger then questioned Ellington as to the "main impulse behind his music" and "as to the technical procedures governing his compositions and the performance of them by his band."[19] The lecture notes reveal that Ellington's answer to the former was "racial", but does not explain further, and, sadly, includes no information on Ellington's response to the latter.

After the lecture and discussion, the Ellington Band performed *Creole Love Call*, *Creole Rhapsody*, and *Tiger Rag*. Then came a wonderful lesson in style. Grainger had the band play a popular tune (not specified in the notes) in two ways—first reading it from the commercially available printed edition, and then "as individualized and specially treated by the Ellington Band."[20] After the band's performance, Ellington played examples of his "piano jazz"—unfortunately the titles of these tunes were not recorded. It is possible that Duke simply treated the class to some improvisations.

To close the lecture, Grainger defined jazz as "being mainly an expression of city life, city moods." For contrast, Grainger performed several Norwegian melodies[21] on the harmonium as "expressive of the purity, loneliness and reserved strength of countrified life." He then pointed out the "need of typical countrified music to balance the large output of city-bred music, as music's contribution to that 'back-to-the-land' movement [is] necessitated, in most civilized countries, by an over-drift of population towards the large cities."[22] (This is a fairly low-key, non-offensive idea for Grainger. It would be interesting to know if the Ellington Band was still in the lecture hall while Grainger played the harmonium!)

Other than a remark that caused Ellington to discover the music of Delius, nothing seems to have come of this meeting between these composer/performers.[23] Yet there are many interesting similarities between these two men, their music, and their compositional philosophies.

Both men were composer/performers—pianists of great talent in their individual styles. Grainger, a concert pianist raised in the conservatory tradition, performed professionally for most of his life. His piano compositions and arrangements were oftentimes so difficult only he could perform them with facility (he referred to these fiendish arrangements as being "dished up" or "rambles on. . ."). His repertoire was deep and varied, and he became somewhat of a champion of Grieg's Piano Concerto in A minor (as well as most of Grieg's other music). He performed it countless times, including a grand tour of Europe in 1909 with Grieg conducting. Ellington's piano instruction contrasted deeply with Grainger's, but produced a performer of equal ability and genius. After a failed attempt at formal piano lessons around age eight, Ellington was mostly self-taught, constantly listening to jazz, ragtime, and honky-tonk pianists in his boyhood Washington D.C. as well as visiting artists.[24] His repertoire, like Grainger's, was extremely wide and varied within his genre. As John Hasse observes, "His style was versatile, ranging from Harlem rent-shouts and down-home blues to poetic prefaces and impressionistic interludes, often laced with dissonant clusters of notes. He could jump instantly from elegant to earthy. And as the years passed, his very personal style of piano playing became more creative and impressive."[25] Both men were born into periods in their respective cultures where music, particularly in the form of a piano in the home, was an expected part of people's lives. And, in the end, the other "hats" they wore as composers, arrangers, and businessmen overshadowed both men's pianistic talents.

They each showed a talent for visual art at an early age. Ellington won a scholarship to study art at the Pratt Institute of Applied Arts in Brooklyn at age 17. Grainger developed an interest in drawing and painting at age 5. He always painted his own Christmas and greeting cards.[26] Both men were talented enough in the visual arts that they had to make a conscious choice while in their teens to pursue music rather than art. And, interestingly enough, this interest in the visual becomes part of both men's musical language—particularly appearing in the titles of Ellington's compositions (*Mood Indigo*, *On a Turquoise Cloud*, *Magenta Haze*, *Transblucency*, etc.)—but also in the wide palette of tone colors both composers enjoyed.

Duke Ellington's mother was a strong force in the development of his personality and philosophies. She was tremendously protective, instilling in him a "confident feeling of being favored for the rest of his life" (most possibly because she had lost her first child in childbirth or infancy.)[27] When she died in the spring of 1935, Ellington could not bring himself to compose for almost half a year. But when he did finally finish *Reminiscing in Tempo*, a reflection on her life and death, it was a real breakthrough composition for him—his longest work of the time (13 minutes), and one that utilized several themes while integrating them into a whole. *Reminiscing in Tempo* and *Symphony in Black* (1934, nine minutes in length) were the first indications that Ellington would not be classified strictly as a "jazz" composer.

Percy Grainger's mother Rose was to "wield such power over the heart and mind of her son that it can be said that from the beginning he was created psychologically in her own image."[28] Sadly, her influences were not limited to the "favored feeling" Ellington's mother provided for him. Among the more distasteful influences on Grainger's person was his mother's insistence that he not mix with children of his own age (adults only), her complete manipulation of his female relationships (platonic and romantic), and her obsession with the blue-eyed, fair-haired, "Nordic" race (a prejudice she had inherited from her mother as well). Grainger's response to her suicide in 1922 was to throw himself into his work. His *The Bride's Tragedy*, performed in Chicago at the Evanston Music Festival one month after her death, was his requiem for her. Unlike Ellington's *Reminiscing in Tempo*, it was not a landmark work for him.

Both men were "instinctive" composers—that is they seemed to gain their compositional knowledge and inspiration from real life and its events. (Neither had much [if any] formal education in composition.) Each composer was grounded in and drew musical inspiration from his own racial background (or in Grainger's case, his philosophically conceived super race). Ellington consistently put his interest in and passion for the history and culture of "his people" forward into his music with works such as *Black, Brown and Beige, Symphony in Black, Harlem, Jump for Joy*, and *My People*. The bulk of Grainger's music celebrated the spirit of what he called the "Nordic" races (defined as Scandinavian, British, Irish, and American). This included a period of collecting folksong (mainly in England) that resulted in countless compositions and their many derivations for different combinations of instruments and voices.

Both composers were revisionists. Grainger often worked on many compositions at once, returning to any one of them a number of times over a period of many years.[29] The very act of composing for Ellington, particularly in the early and middle years, involved revision in the form of sectionalized ideas that could be moved into various sequences—the order in which ideas were composed was not necessarily the order of the finished composition. This was connected to the "democratic" method Ellington had of composing with the band in front of him—each performer had an opportunity to put in their own musical ideas and nuances. Ellington also had a penchant for revising masterworks such as *The Mooche, Mood Indigo*, and *Diminuendo in Blue/Crescendo in Blue*. And of course, each recording the band made of the same work could be considered a revision.

Ellington and Grainger were pioneers, constantly experimenting, never particularly concerned with the main stream of music in their respective genres. Grainger said he was the only composer he knew "who has not been affected by fashion or modes."[30] He viewed the symphony orchestra as an outdated relic of the nineteenth century and resented that composers of his generation felt they must write for this medium simply because it was considered the most important. Ellington's sound was always different from the mainstream of jazz, whatever that happened to be at any given time. Even the tidal wave of Swing did not greatly affect Ellington's compositional style (granted there were a few nods in that direction, both satirical and serious). As a composer of truly "new" music, Ellington's sound was always ahead of its time—for example, pieces like *Cottontail* and *Mainstem* that foretell the rhythmic phrasing and angular melodies of bop. Since neither composer was in the musical mainstream, both suffered a lack of acceptance in "serious" music circles until fairly recently.

Although we can only guess what Grainger thought of the music the Ellington Band performed in his class on that October afternoon, the above similarities may indicate a connection. Certainly, if the two composers knew at least some of the other's work, there would have been an ability to understand, appreciate, and respect it.

A look at the pieces the Ellington Band performed that day, using Grainger's definitions of their musical characteristics, might reveal why this music appealed to the classical composer enough to include it in his lectures (even in the early 1930's, this would have been seen as controversial). Aspects of two tunes played that day, *Creole Love Call* (1927) and *Creole Rhapsody* (1931), can be compared to Grainger's *Lincolnshire Posy* (1937), a work considered by many to be his masterpiece.

All three compositions reflect the composers' interest in their own "racial music." The two Ellington works portray cultural aspects of African Americans (although, according to John Hasse, Ellington was never in Creole country before composing the works). *Creole Rhapsody* was awarded the best composition of the year from the New York School of Music in 1933—chosen "because it portrayed the Negro life as no other piece had."[31] Grainger's *Lincolnshire Posy* is a collection of folk tunes recorded in the field (from Lincolnshire, England) as he sought to honor the singers of his "blue-eyed" culture.

Creole Love Call's unique sound is derived for the most part from the beautiful, wordless vocals of Adelaide Hall that become a part of the instrumental texture. Hall transforms her voice in several ways, often imitating the growl trumpet sounds of Bubber Miley (now listed as co-composer with Ellington and clarinetist Rudy Jackson). This idea is an interesting reversal of Grainger's observation that Ellington's music includes the "imitation of the human voice by instruments." The combination of her haunting vocal line and the opening clarinet trio certainly creates a "rapturous mood", one of the "high emotional and technical qualities" in Ellington's music Grainger observes, not to mention the clarinet trio when it shifts into altissimo register. Miley, Jackson and Hall's solos qualify as "display music (virtuosity)" and "rhapsodic improvisation by individual players of the orchestra"—all with hints of the New Orleans sound. And the "gliding and off-pitch sounds in jazz" are everywhere—even in the call and response between woodwinds and brass. In this composition in blues form, all of the above techniques create, as Grainger observes, "sustained melodiousness."

Lincolnshire Posy was a commission from the American Bandmasters' Association for their annual Grand Concert and Convention at Milwaukee in March, 1937. Grainger compiled a suite of six arrangements of folksongs he had collected previously (as early as 1905). Three of the movements were composed from scratch in the rather frantic period of four days. The work is:

> Dedicated to the old folksingers who sang so sweetly to me. Indeed, each number is intended to be a kind of musical portrait of the singer who sang its underlying melody—a musical portrait of the singer's personality no less than of his habits of song—his regular or irregular wonts of rhythm, his preference for gaunt or ornately arabesqued delivery, his contrasts of legato and staccato, his tendency towards breadth or delicacy of tone.[32]

This last statement reveals a detail of composition that Ellington utilized constantly—that of composing for the members of his band that he knew so well— tailoring his material to their strengths and weaknesses, thereby reflecting their musical personalities.

Grainger recorded the melodic material for the third movement, *Rufford Park Poachers,* in 1906—sung by Joseph Taylor of Saxby-All-Saints, Lincolnshire. Its opening flurry of meter changes, treatment of the material in canon, and free-sounding rhythms create a "rhapsodic improvisatory" sound. The connection with "imitation of the human voice by instruments" is obvious. Grainger prepared two separate opening sections of this movement scored for different pairs of instruments (both versions are highly colored timbres). He preferred Version B, as it features the soprano saxophone, "that is, if its player has assurance enough to throb forth this melody with searching, piercing prominence."[33] Grainger was a great proponent of the saxophone family, particularly the soprano saxophone, claiming they produced the sound closest to the human voice. "Gliding and off-pitch" sounds are created by the use of written-out glissandos, grace notes, short trills and turns, muted and stopped sounds, and directions to the players such as "nasal." The opening section creates a haunting, beautiful "rapturous mood" using "sustained melodiousness" that is similar to *Creole Rhapsody* (granted somewhat more polyphonic). And, although the solo lines in the canon are written out, the performers create the sound of "display music" or improvisation in the execution of the difficult opening section.

Creole Rhapsody was Ellington's first extended work. At six minutes (somewhat dictated by the length of two sides of a 78-rpm disc) it anticipates the longer single-movement works and suites that have become such an important part of Ellington's repertoire.[34] Ironically, although the sounds of "rhapsodic improvisation by individual players of the orchestra" are heard everywhere, Ellington composed most of the solo work.[35] (It would be interesting to know if Grainger was aware of this when he led the class discussion before the band performed regarding art music [fixed notation] versus free improvisation [see above].) Three themes, each with their own tempo (an innovation of the time) alternate and unite the work. There is an unusual interlude played by Johnny Hodges at "double time" tempo that occurs right before an interesting treatment of the third theme—played in a free-rhythm style in conversation between Ellington and clarinetist Barney Bigard. The contrast provided in the three themes—minor and driving, relaxed blues, and beautifully sweet and peaceful—allow for more than one "mood" in the same composition. The textures are clear and balanced—again something Grainger would have been delighted with (he stated again in his preparatory lecture what he had previously written in *The Etude*; that the "balance of tone" in a jazz band is more perfect than the finest symphony orchestra).

Several of the "high emotional and technical qualities" Grainger applied to Ellington's music can be discovered in other movements of his *Lincolnshire Posy*. Like *Creole Rhapsody*, Grainger often changes mood within a single movement, for example the fierce entrance of the *Duke of Marlboro Fanfare* into the calm, lilting texture of the first movement, *Lisbon*; or the change from brash to playful to mysteriously impressionistic in *Lord Melbourne*; and the contrasting statements of each variation in *Lost Lady Found*. A delightful passage in the fourth movement, *The Brisk Young Sailor*, uses a double-time figure (in piccolo, flutes, E♭ clarinet and first B♭ clarinets) to accompany the melody—creating the same intense energy that Johnny Hodges's solo statement does in *Creole Rhapsody*. The opening section of *Lord Melbourne* (which returns twice in abbreviated form) is composed in traditional notation, but set in free time. Grainger explains to the conductor, "In the passages marked 'Free Time'. . . the Bandleader should vary his note-lengths with that rhythmic elasticity so characteristic of many English folksingers. . . give free reign to his rhythmic fancy, just as folksingers do. Each note with an arrow above it may be beaten with a down beat . . ."[36] This concept, so much a part of the jazz music presented in his lecture (like the free section between Ellington and Bigard in *Creole Rhapsody* and the concept of improvisation) caused problems at the premiere of *Lincolnshire Posy*:

> To his great disappointment the ensuing performance at the convention was a fiasco. The bandsmen found the irregular and "free" rhythms of two of the movements so difficult that these pieces had to be dropped from the final concert. Grainger remarked later "they were keener on their beer than on their music." Fortunately the work was performed three months later by the Goldman Band with complete success and this worthy bunch of musicians restored his faith in its practicality.[37]

Although *Creole Rhapsody* is regarded as Ellington's first extended piece, he did record a two-sided version of *Tiger Rag* with Brunswick in 1929 (two years before *Creole Rhapsody*). It is not clear which version of *Tiger Rag* the band performed in Grainger's class. But the 1929 recording reveals a barn-burning version that has in profusion what the other two compositions that Ellington performed that day do not—polyphony. The selection of these three particular Ellington tunes allowed Grainger to illustrate all his points regarding his "nutshell" definition of Ellington's music.

There is no indication that the two ever met again. Nor is there any record of what either man thought about their one encounter. Grainger quickly grew disappointed with academic life. He taught through summer session, and then left in August, 1933. He never accepted another academic position (though many were offered) and even rejected offers of honorary degrees from several American universities. Ellington was on the brink of one of the most creative and successful periods in his career—a career that would include numerous awards, honorary academic degrees, and the Presidential Medal of Freedom.

It is not clear if Ellington was ever aware of Grainger's more offensive philosophies on race and music. If he was, there appears to be no record of his reaction—he may have chosen to ignore them and accept the opportunity to further his music and career in performing at NYU.[38] This would have been consistent with similar decisions he made throughout his career. There is also no record that Grainger made any racially offensive statements during the composers' time together. This may indicate sincere respect for the music he was presenting to his students.

There is no doubt that when the two men's work is compared they share many musical similarities, including unusual mixtures of instruments, a love of highly colored timbres, and, above all, melody. Along with other composers of the era, they were interested in developing music that was representative of their ethnic roots. If at the start of the twenty-first century Grainger's racially inspired musical concepts seem simple-minded, misguided, or deeply offensive, they are an extreme manifestation of ideas that influenced many composers at the time. Ellington's "racial music" philosophies were more positively oriented—building up and holding up his own "people" to the rest of the world:

> We are children of the sun and our race has a definite tradition of beauty and glory and vitality that is as rich and powerful as the sun itself. These traditions are ours to express, and will enrich our careers in proportion to the sincerity and faithfulness with which we interpret them.[39]

In spite of shared ideas of the role of music in culture, race, and new music, as well as many musical characteristics, ultimately, it is the distinctive character of each of these two men that gives their music its individual qualities.

Irving Mills, Percy Grainger and Duke Ellington

Lecture – Oct. 25th 1932 –

question of balance in Chamber music & ... Orchestra – number of instruments –

record of *Creole love call* – ask yourself is
this polyphonic or not –

P.G. introduces Duke Ellington

plays 1st Creole love call –

2nd Creole rhapsody –

An extra number – Tiger Rag (wild one)

Ellington plays piano solo –

→ After this orchestra left – B. played :
Sparre Olsen's: Byggdeviser fraa Lom –
Grieg's: Niels Tallefjorden.

mentions Ole Bull's "Sæterjentens Söndag" –

P.G. & Rogers play arr. by J. Svensens string

(virtuosity) in Chopin
Delius & pre-Bach music (statement (6). The gliding & off-pitch 16
sounds in jazz considered an important step towards the
"Free music" of the future (Statements 1, 3, 17).

X Duke Ellington questioned by the lecturer as to the main
impulse (Ellington declared it to be "racial") behind his music
& as to the technical procedures governing his compositions
& the performance of them by his band.
            Musical Illustrations by
            Duke Ellington & his Jazz Orchestra:
"Creole Love Call", "Creole Rhapsody", "Tiger-Rag" etc.
The orchestra also played a popular tune
in two ways: (1) reading it from the printed edition,
(2) as individualized & specially treated by the Ellington
band.
Duke Ellington also played examples of his piano jazz.
At the close of the D. Ellington demonstrations the
lecturer defined such music (jazz) as being mainly
an expression of city life, city moods.   As a contrast
the lecturer played on the piano & harmonium.
    Ole Bull: Saeterjentens Söndag (The dairymaid's Sunday)
    Grieg: Niels Tallefjoren (from op 17)

Handwritten notes, October 25, 1932

C. Scott: Slow movement from Quintet for piano and strings (example of gliding intonation).

Lecture V, October 18, 1932

Bach's Fantasias compared with the Fantasies heard at the last lecture (Statement 8).

The reintroduction of the tenor part as the main tune-bearing voice in Brahms, perhaps owing to his knowledge of pre-Bach and midieval music. Is Syncopation more evident in Jazz than in Brahms? (Statement 17) Syncopations in British and American (white) folksongs cited as the probable forerunners of syncopation in Ragtime and Jazz (Statement 17).

Preparation for next lecture, when Duke Ellington's Jazz Band will illustrate: Quotations from article on Duke Ellington in "Disques", in which Ellington's and Delius's music are linked together. High emotional and technical qualities in D. Ellington's music -- rapturous moods, sustained melodiousness, imitation of human voice by instruments, polyphonic texture, rhapsodic improvisation by individual players of the orchestra.

Musical Illustrations

Bach - (Liszt): Organ Fantasia and Fugue, G Minor (played on piano)
Syncopations and other rhythmic dislocations in Brahms:
A Minor and G Minor Capriccios
Paganini and Handel Variations (all for piano).

Tenor-part Melodies in Brahms:
        Intermezzo, Op. 117 No. 3; Romance in F, Op. 118 (piano)
        "The Rainbow", English folk song, sung by the lecturer.

Moods in Delius and Duke Ellington compared:
        Record of Delius's "The Walk to the Paradise Garden".
        Record of D. Ellington's "Creole Love Call" and "Creole Rhapsody".

Lecture VI, October 25, 1932

Discussion of Duke Ellington's music before it is played.

Art Music defined as music fixed by notation -- to what extent is Ellington's music art music (fixed by notation), to what extent does it admit free improvisation (varying with each performance) by individual players? Balance of tone (3 clarinets, 3 trumpets, 3 saxophones, etc.) declared more perfect in such a jazz band than in the finest symphony orchestras. Top-heaviness and bad balance in symphony orchestras explained (Statement 7). Ellington's Jazz declared to combine many various elements of "classical" music: Polyphony, chambermusic, refine-

10

Notes October 18, 1932

ment of tone, display-music (virtuosity) as in Chopin and Liszt,
rapturous mood as in Delius and pre-Bach music (Statement 16).
The gliding and off-pitch sounds in jazz considered an important step to
the Free Music of the future (Statements 1, 3, 17).

Duke Ellington questioned by the lecturer as to the main impulse behind
his music (Ellington declared it to be "racial") and as to the technical procedures governing his compositions and the performance of
them by his band.

                    Musical Illustrations by
                    Duke Ellington and his Jazz Orchestra:

"Creole Love Call", "Creole Rhapsody", "Tiger-Rag", etc. The Orchestra
also played a popular tune in two ways: (1) reading it from the usual
commercial printed edition, (2) as individualized and specially treated
by the Ellington Band.

Duke Ellington also played examples of his piano jazz. At the close
of the D. Ellington demonstrations the lecturer defined such music
(jazz) as being mainly an expression of city life, city moods. As a
contrast the lecturer played on the piano and harmonium

          Ole Bull: Saeterjentens Sondag (The Dairymaid's Sunday)
          Grieg   : Niels Tallefjoren (From Op. 17)
          Sparre Olsen: Peasant Songs from Lom (Norsk Musik Forlag,
                                                       Oslo)

as expressive of the purity, loneliness and reserved strength of countrified life and pointed out the need of typical countrified music
(to balance the large output of city-bred music) as music's contribution to that "back-to-the-land" movement necessitated, in most civilized countries, by an over-drift of population towards the large
cities.

                    Lecture VII, Nov.1, 1932.

    Artistic impulses (choice, taste) & anti-artistic conventions (habit,
    fashion); we should none of us be afraid, out of conventionality, to
    apply our individual taste to the critisism of conventionally accepte
    "masterpieces".

    Was Beethoven in his slow movements capable of sustaining a solemn
    mood, a calm, lofty musical type, without drifting off into dramatic
    contrasts, passage-work, display-music, comic relief & various forms
    of irritability, restlessness & frivolousness ? (See Lecture VIII).
    Was Goethe's opinion of Beethoven's music (that it represented the
    sentimentality & esthetic disintegration of his age) not justified,
    in the light of our grander & more spiritual 20th century conception
    of music? Perhaps the "industrial revolution", and the misery and

                              11

Notes October 25, 1932

NEW YORK UNIVERSITY
COLLEGE OF FINE ARTS

Music A---- A Study of the Manifold Nature of Music
FINAL EXAMINATION**Tuesday, Jan.17,1933
4-7 Room 703
Associate Professor Percy Grainger

I. What are the main characteristics of melody (if by "melody" we mean something more sustained,more vocal,more rapturous,than by the terms "tune"
"theme" "motiv") as we find it in primitive music,in folk-music,in
oriental art-music and in European art-music?

II. From what place and period comes the statement:"Poetry is the expression
of earnest thought and singing is the prolonged utterance of that expression"?

III. Name the two main types of rhythm.

IV. Name some "cumulative" composers,in whose compositions the accumulated
traditions of many periods of musical culture are preserved and blended
into a complex whole.

V. Name some "experimental" composers whose compositions contain such experiments as the following (or kindred experiments):-
    (a) the introduction of the dominant-seventh chord
    (b) irregular rhythms caused by applying to French verse the principles
        of Latin verse
    (c) rehearsal-room mistakes and "nature-sounds" introduced into art-
        music
    (d) irregular rhythms in 20th century music
    (e) atonalism or disharmony
    (f) intervals closer than the half-tone

VI. Name some "modish" composers-those who compose mainly in the prevailing
styles of their time,without reaching out far into the past or the
future.

VII. Classify G.de Machaut,Monteverdi,Palestrina,Claude le Jeune,William
Lawes,Purcell,Bach,Haydn,Handel,Beethoven,Wagner,Richard Strauss,
Brahms,Cesar Franck,Gabriel Faure,Tchaikovsky,Scriabin,Debussy,Cyril
Scott,Ernest Bloch,Wallingford Riegger,Stravinsky,Arnold Schönberg,
Frederick Delius,Arthur Fickenscher in relation to questions 4,5,6.
[Write as follows:Such and such composers belong under 4,5. Such
amd such composers belong under 6).

VIII. Give your personal definition of originality in musical composition.

IX. Name some main influences in Debussy's music.

X. What type of folk-music or primitive music mainly inspired Balakirew's
"Tamara" and "Islamey" and Rimsky-Korsakov's "Scheherazade"?

XI. What chiefly distinguishes Jazz from Ragtime?

XII. In what respects may Jazz(such as Duke Ellington's and Paul Whiteman's)
be described as "the most classical of popular musics"?

25

— Grainger Museum

Final Exam, January 17, 1933

DISCOGRAPHY

Delius, Frederick. *The Walk to the Paradise Garden* on *Delius Orchestral Works*. Orchestra of Welsh National Opera conducted by Sir Charles Mackerras. [London]: Decca 289 460 290-2, [1990]. Compact disc.

Ellington, Duke. *Tiger Rag* on *Early Ellington*. The Duke Ellington Orchestra. [New York]: Decca Jazz GRD-3-640, [1994]. Compact disc.

Ellington, Duke. *Creole Rhapsody* on *The Duke Ellington Centennial Edition: The Complete RCA Victor Recordings* (1927-1973). [New York]: BMG Classics 09026-63386-2, [1999]. Compact disc.

Grainger, Percy. *Lincolnshire Posy*. Eastman Wind Ensemble conducted by Frederick Fennell. [New York]: Mercury 432 754-2, [1991]. Compact disc.

BIBLIOGRAPHY

Balough, Teresa, ed. *Percy Aldridge Grainger: A Musical Genius from Australia*. Nedlands: CIRCME, 1997.

Bird, John. *Percy Grainger*. Oxford: Oxford University Press, 1999.

Callaway, Frank, ed. *Percy Aldridge Grainger Symposium*. Nedlands: CIRCME, 1997.

Darrell, R.D. "Black Beauty." In *The Duke Ellington Reader*, ed. Mark Tucker, 57-65. New York: Oxford University Press, 1993.

Ellington, Duke. "From Where I Lie." In *The Duke Ellington Reader*, ed. Mark Tucker, 131. New York: Oxford University Press, 1993.

Ellington, Mercer and Stanley Dance. *Duke Ellington in Person: An Intimate Memoir*. Boston: Houghton Mifflin Company, 1978.

Gillies, Malcolm and David Pear, ed. *The All-Round Man: Selected Letters of Percy Grainger 1914–1961*. Oxford: Clarendon Press, 1994.

Grainger, Percy. "What Effect if Jazz Likely to Have Upon the Music of the Future?" *The Etude*, September, 1927, p. 593-94.

_____. *Lincolnshire Posy*, 1987. SBS-250. Cleveland: Ludwig Music Publishing Co., Inc., 1987. Score.

_____. Lecture notes, photo reproduction, and final examination. The Grainger Museum, The University of Melbourne. Faxed documents.

Hasse, John. Curator of American Music, National Museum of American History, Smithsonian Institution. Electronic mail correspondence, March 18, 2002.

Hasse, John Edward. *Beyond Category: The Life and Genius of Duke Ellington*. New York: Da Capo Press, 1993.

Lewis, Thomas P., ed. *A Source Guide to the Music of Percy Grainger*. White Plains: Pro Am Music Resource, Inc., 1991.

Mellers, Wilfrid. *Percy Grainger*. New York: Oxford University Press, 1992.

The New Grove Dictionary of Music and Musicians. S.v. "Percy Grainger," by Malcolm Gillies and David Pear.

_____. S.v. "Duke Ellington," by Andre Hodeir and Gunther Schuller.

_____. S.v. "Frederick Delius," by Anthony Payne.

Nicholson, Stuart. *Reminiscing in Tempo: A Portrait of Duke Ellington*. Boston: Northern University Press, 1999.

Peachment, Amelia. Assistant Curator, Grainger Museum, Information Division, The University of Melbourne. Electronic mail correspondence, February—March, 2002.

Simon, Robert. *Percy Grainger: The Pictorial Biography*. Winston-Salem: SD Publications, 1987.

Tucker, Mark, ed. *The Duke Ellington Reader*. New York: Oxford University Press, 1993.

Tucker, Mark. "The Renaissance Education of Duke Ellington." In *Black Music in the Harlem Renaissance: A Collection of Essays*, ed. Samuel A. Floyd, Jr., 1990.

NOTES

[1] John Hasse, Curator of American Music at the Smithsonian Institution. E-mail dated 18 March 2002.

[2] An advertising manual compiled by Irving Mills' office in 1934 that was sent to theater and ballroom managers   contains several references to Percy Grainger and claims that Basil Cameron (British conductor of the Seattle Symphony) was also present when Ellington performed at NYU.

Stuart Nicholson, *Reminiscing in Tempo: A Portrait of Duke Ellington* (Boston: Northern University Press, 1999), 152-159.

[3] Mercer Ellington with Stanley Dance, *Duke Ellington in Person: An Intimate Memoir*(Boston: Houghton Mifflin Company, 1978), 38.

[4] John Bird, *Percy Grainger* (Oxford: Oxford University Press, 1999), 80.

[5] Wilfrid Mellers, *Percy Grainger* (Oxford: Oxford University Press, 1992), 60-61.

[6] Percy Grainger, "What Effect is Jazz Likely to Have Upon the Music of the Future?" *The Etude*, September, 1924, pp. 593-4.

[7] Ibid

[8] Percy Grainger, "What Effect is Jazz Likely to Have Upon the Music of the Future?" *The Etude*, September, 1924, pp. 593-4.

[9] Percy Grainger, Letter to D.C. Parker, April 26, 1933, in *The All-Round Man: Selected letters of Percy Grainger 1914-1961*, ed. Malcolm Gillies and David Pear (Oxford: Clarendon Press, 1994), 117.

[10] Percy Grainger's lecture notes, Grainger Museum, University of Melbourne.

[11] According to Grainger biographer John Bird, Grainger told Ellington this, which puzzled Ellington as he did not know of Delius or his music. Ellington was curious enough to investigate, and discovered he enjoyed Delius' music - although he was never convinced of Grainger's suggested similarities between the two composers.

[12] According to Delius scholar Anthony Payne, Grainger's *Hill Songs* and chromatic folksong arrangements had a marked influence on Delius' middle period, including his *A Song of the High Hills* (1911).

[13] John Bird, *Percy Grainger* (Oxford: Oxford University Press, 1999), 239-40.

[14] Percy Grainger's lecture notes, Grainger Museum, University of Melbourne.

[15] Anthony Payne, "Frederick Delius," in *The New Grove Dictionary of Music and Musicians*.

[16] Percy Grainger's lecture notes, Grainger Museum, University of Melbourne.

[17] Ibid. These comparisons to European art music composers reveal again that Grainger thought of Ellington's music within a European context - very different than Ellington's own views.

[18] The scope of Grainger's Free Music and Free Music machines is too large for this paper. He worked on these ideas, compositions, and, in collaboration with Burnett Cross, actual machines from the early 1930's to the end of his life. The Free Music concept is music whose melody, rhythm and texture are liberated from the traditional constraints of scale, beat and harmony.

[19] Percy Grainger's lecture notes, Grainger Museum, University of Melbourne.

[20] Ibid.

[21] Ole Bull's *The Dairymaid's Sunday,* Sparre Olsen's *Peasant Songs from Lom*, and Grieg's *Niels Tallsfjoren* from Opus 17.

[22] Percy Grainger's lecture notes, Grainger Museum, University of Melbourne.

[23] Several sources contend that Ellington did investigate Delius' music and liked it.

[24] Ellington biographer John Hasse divides these players into the "unschooled"—Ralph Green, Shrimp Bronner, Lester Dishman, Clarence Bower, Sticky Mack, Blind Johnny, and The Man with a Thousand Fingers; and the "ones who could read music" - Claude Hopkins, Roscoe Lee, Gertie Wells, Doc Perry, Louis Brown, and Louis Thomas.

[25] John Hasse, *Beyond Category: The Life and Genius of Duke Ellington* (New York: Da Capo Press, 1993), 316.

[26] John Bird, *Percy Grainger* (Oxford: Oxford University Press, 1999), 15.

[27] John Hasse, *Beyond Category: The Life and Genius of Duke Ellington* (New York: Da Capo Press, 1993), 22-23.

[28] John Bird, *Percy Grainger* (Oxford: Oxford University Press, 1999), 7.

[29] Ibid, 303.

[30] Percy Grainger, Letter to D.C. Parker, April 26, 1933, in *The All-Round Man: Selected letters of Percy Grainger 1914-1961*, ed. Malcolm Gillies and David Pear (Oxford: Clarendon Press, 1994), 120.

[31] John Hasse, *Beyond Category: The Life and Genius of Duke Ellington* (New York: Da Capo Press, 1993), 165.

[32] Percy Grainger, program notes for *Lincolnshire Posy* from *A Source Guide to the Music of Percy Grainger*, ed. Thomas P. Lewis (White Plains: Pro Am Music Resources, Inc., 1991), 196.

[33] Percy Grainger, note to bandleaders in score, *Lincolnshire Posy*, 1987. SBS-250 (Cleveland: Ludwig Music Publishing Company Inc., 1987).

[34] Comments refer to the second version recorded for Victor in June, 1931 which is markedly different than the first recording for Brunswick earlier that same year.

[35] John Hasse, *Beyond Category: The Life and Genius of Duke Ellington* (New York: Da Capo Press, 1993), 188.

[36] Percy Grainger, "Lincolnshire Posy," 1987. SBS-250 (Cleveland: Ludwig Music Publishing Company Inc., 1987).

[37] John Bird, *Percy Grainger* (Oxford: Oxford University Press, 1999), 250.

[38] The author was unable to travel to the Smithsonian to search in detail for specific mention of this meeting. Curator John Hasse believes there are press releases that cover the event - possibly there are Ellington's thoughts and reactions as well. The Grainger Museum in Melbourne provided the sum of its information, which was only several pages.

[39] Duke Ellington, "From Where I Lie" in *The Duke Ellington Reader*, ed. Mark Tucker (New York: Oxford University Press, 1993), 131.

The Goldman Era

Edwin Franko Goldman and Erik Leidzén: Musical Partnership and Friendship, 1933–1956 *by Ronald W. Holz*

During the period 1933–1956, Edwin Franko Goldman (1878–1956) and Erik Leidzén (1894–1962) maintained a professional relationship that resulted in a remarkable output of music for wind band, the majority of it written for and premiered by the Goldman Band of New York City. Leidzén served as Goldman's principal arranger throughout these 23 years, supplying a critically acclaimed series of transcriptions, arrangements, and original compositions. At the same time, he also arranged and scored at least 50 of Goldman's marches, including the revised concert version of *On the Mall*. A lasting friendship developed within this same time period that enhanced their collaborations, and many in the wider band community of America benefited by their interaction.[1]

When Goldman turned 70, New Year's Day 1948, Leidzén wrote "A Clover-Leaf of Sonnets" in honor of his "boss." In the following two excerpts from these sonnets, Leidzén provides an engaging verse portrait of this giant of American music in the context of an evening at the Central Park band shell. It helps evoke the Goldman era, while summarizing Goldman's achievements:

> The night is warm; from somewhere in the dark
> Comes honeysuckle-fragrance – it is June;
> The aspen-leaf is motionless; the moon
> Sheds silver on the silent scene; but hark!
> From the illumined concave shell there comes
> The pleasant sound of music clear and bright:
> An overture the Goldman Band intones.
> Reverberating rhythms from rumbling drums
> Roll gaily festive through the summer night
> To stirring strains from trumpets and trombones.
>
> At three-score years and ten you stand erect
> And wield your magic wand with steady hand.
> Your snow-white head, well-known throughout the land,
> Commands our admiration and respect.
> With courage you have ventured to select
> Only the best in music for your band.
> The standards you have set are high and grand;
> Your sterling worth and stature they reflect.
> Long may you exercise benevolent
> And beneficent influence in the sphere
> In which you move, your chosen branch of art....[2]

E.F. Goldman and Erik Leidzén first met in the spring of 1930 when they served on a team of judges for a national band composition contest the Salvation Army [SA] held in its 50th anniversary year in America. Leidzén at this time was one of the few hired professionals in that denomination; he coordinated the SA's music program in the New York Metropolitan area. Goldman's initial involvement with the SA probably came through two sources. First, John Philip Sousa, who had been commissioned to write a march for the SA's May 1930 national anniversary celebrations in New York City, may have enlisted his participation. Second, it may also have been SA cornet virtuoso John Allan, a former cornet student of Goldman, who by this time, was a high ranking SA clergyman.[3]

The next documented interaction between Goldman and Leidzén came exactly three years later. On 26 May, 1933, E.F. Goldman was invited as the guest of honor at the Finale Music Festival of the SA's Friday Evening at the Temple meeting series at 120 West 14th Street, Manhattan. During the concert Goldman led several mass band and choir items. At the climactic moment in the concert, Leidzén presented to Goldman the score of a new march, *EFG*, a short compositional tour-de-force based on Goldman's initials. The outstanding 9-piece Metropolitan Brass Ensemble premiered the march, and Goldman declared Leidzén to be a "band genius."[4]

Ironically, at this same event Leidzén ran afoul of SA National Commander Evangeline Booth. Leidzén felt his honor and professional integrity compromised and he felt compelled to submit his resignation, not an easy decision in the midst of the Depression. Despite some efforts towards reconciliation, the breach was not healed for many years. Leidzén's alienation from The Salvation Army is what led him into a career as a wind band arranger and composer.

E.F. Goldman fully recognized Leidzén's many talents and, by the fall of 1933, Goldman was hiring Leidzén for some small arranging jobs. The initial projects were several piano transcriptions of Goldman marches. On a copy of the published piano version of *On the Mall* Goldman wrote in the upper right hand corner "You've done a fine job with this."[5] Goldman subsequently increased the amount and scope of Leidzén's work load by giving him the role of 'associate editor' for the two-volume *Goldman Band System* published by Carl Fischer in 1935. In this band method book Goldman demonstrated how to achieve many of the goals he outlined in *Band Betterment*, a book released one year earlier.[6]

About this same time Mayhew Lake (or Mike Lake as he preferred) was taking on more work in addition to his responsibilities as editor-in-chief of band and orchestral music at Carl Fischer (1913–1948). Leidzén then was the ideal choice to step in as Goldman's new "right hand man" in arranging, something Lake had done for many years. Lake also recommended that Leidzén assume his teaching responsibilities at Ernest Williams' School of Music, a position which led to Leidzén ghost-writing a great deal of music for Williams, including the *C Minor Symphony for Band*. Several of Ernest Williams' star pupils also studied composition with Leidzén, including Leonard B. Smith, later renowned as director of the Detroit Concert Band.[7] A brief hiatus took place, however, in the Goldman/Leidzén collaboration, when in the summer and fall of 1934, Leidzén returned to Sweden in an attempt to sort through exactly what his career path should be. When he arrived back in Manhattan in January 1935 Leidzén was ready to work more completely with, and for, Edwin Franko Goldman.

It is fortunate that Leidzén was a meticulous record keeper, especially for income tax purposes, and by reviewing his account books and contracts that survive either in the Salvation Army's National Archives or in the Goldman Collection at the University of Iowa, much can be learned about the Goldman/Leidzén partnership.[8] The first page in Leidzén's account notebook under the column for works commissioned by EFG for 1935–36 is shown on page 107. The pieces listed here were among Leidzén's first projects for the Goldman Band and included two arrangements of Bach compositions, *Come Sweet Death* and *Jesu Joy of Man's Desiring* – the latter listed as "Chorale 147." Longer transcriptions included the finale from Dvorak's *New World Symphony*, and the *Coronation Scene* from Mussorgsky's opera *Boris Godunov*. Also cited here is his first band arrangement of a Goldman march, *Chimes of Liberty*, followed by the marches *America*, and *Bugles and Drums*.

On the next page of the notebook, a common entry is evidenced, a march without title—just above the name Mussorgsky; then, Leidzén lists the various portions of *Pictures at an Exhibition* that had been ordered by Goldman. This unnamed march is probably a Goldman march.

Additional listings are more explicit, as indicated several years later (see page 108). Included among items arranged for the 1942, 1943, and 1944 seasons of the Goldman Band, there are multiple unnamed marches. Notice on these pages a whole group of Goldman marches; several are listed as March A or March B (December 1942, for 1943 season), some with no name at all, and others identified by title, like *Anniversary March*. I have identified 17 of these unnamed marches in Leidzén's records that survive or are legible. Therefore, it is difficult to determine an accurate count for the number of Goldman marches Leidzén arranged or rearranged, though we definitely know that Leidzén was involved with at least 50 of the just over 100 marches attributed to Goldman. In addition, not all Goldman marches arranged by Erik Leidzén bear that information in published form. The most famous omission is that of *On the Mall*, a march that went through substantive changes when Goldman and Leidzén revisited the initial Goldman—Lake version.[9]

In 1935, Leidzén charged the modest price of $1.50 per page of band score, regardless of the project, so Goldman had a rare bargain and a very ethical partner. This fee would gradually rise as Leidzén's stature grew parallel with Goldman's esteem. The other thing we find from these records is that in some instances Goldman made decisions in advance before assigning a work. For example, the initial movements ordered of the *Pictures at an Exhibition* transcription, clearly show that Goldman did not assign the entire work. He purposefully ignored movements that might be seen to be mean spirited, in bad taste, or more importantly, anti-Semitic, an affront to his Jewish identity. Thus, in the Leidzén transcription of Pictures, there is no (#1) *Gnome* or dwarf, or (#6) *Samuel Goldenberg and Schmuyle*. There are also times when Goldman's son Richard did the musicological research to provide Leidzén with the best edition or manuscript source available for the work requested – a case in point is the Wagner *Trauersinfonie* transcription. When discussing Leidzén's arranging, transcribing, or composing achievements, one must bear in mind whether a work was designed for the high professional level of the Goldman Band, more general consumption of the public at large, or bands in the public schools. On close examination, a marked difference can be discerned.[10]

The contracts between Goldman and Leidzén that survive from this period are sometimes for single pieces, as in the extant copy from 1939 for the Rimsky-Korsakov *Procession of the Nobles*. The publication contract indicates that Leidzén had previously received "sufficient" dollars by supplying the arrangement for the Goldman Band concert season! Sometimes the contract (see page 111) was for a grouping of works, as in this sample found in the Goldman Collection which contained three classical transcriptions designed for the 1937 season of the Goldman Band, plus a set of six cornet solos for Goldman's publishing concern and a set not published with Leidzén's name on the score.

One also has to be careful of the chronology involved as seen in the Leidzén account notebooks. Please note the entry for the "new arrangement" of On the Mall but also the initial completion of *Procession of the Nobles*, here called the Cortege from the opera *Mlada*, which was written for the 1938 season of the Goldman Band. On page 110 we saw the contract releasing *Procession of the Nobles* to Goldman for publication, in 1939.

Goldman first featured an original composition by Leidzén with the Goldman Band in the 1935 season. The piece, *Fugue with Chorale*, was also performed in 1936 in its orchestral version by Howard Hanson and the Rochester Civic Orchestra. The basis of the piece was a Swedish funeral hymn, which Goldman insisted be included in the *Goldman Band System* books. In successive years, Leidzén had an original work on the Goldman concert series nearly every year until Goldman's death; and in some years there were multiple original works. Among these early standards of the concert band repertoire were; the *First Swedish Rhapsody*, a ghostwritten Symphony for Ernest Williams, a Leidzén series of overtures, chorale preludes like *Doxology*. Lesser known, and still unpublished, were original works specially designed to showcase the talented players of the Goldman Band. In 1939 Goldman asked for just such a piece, *Band Virtuosities*, perhaps better titled Variations for Symphonic Band on Franz Schubert's *Lied*, 'The Trout.' It is in many ways a "Young Person's Guide to the Wind Band" and premiered several years before Benjamin Britten's famous composition. The manuscript score and parts for this work are in the Goldman Collection at Iowa State University, Iowa City, Iowa.[11]

Beginning about the 1936 summer season, Goldman on occasion asked Leidzén to conduct the Band, a rare honor at that time. The relationship between the two men was becoming more trustful, though in correspondence of the late 1930s and early 40s the tone is still formal: "Dear Sir…Dear Mr. Leidzén…Dear Dr. Goldman."[12] Not to be forgotten also is the importance of EFG's son, Richard Franko Goldman. Richard may be considered the chief guiding and advisory force behind much that EFG attempted and achieved during the last 20 years of his career. Richard became a good friend to Erik, and records indicate he took lessons in band scoring and arranging from Leidzén. One entry in the Leidzén account books shows eleven lessons at $3/hour.[13] One can only imagine the shared energy and vision for a renewed band culture in America these three men held—dynamic band entrepreneur and successful conductor/entertainer EFG, scholarly musicologist/theorist Richard, and Erik Leidzén, composer, arranger, and skilled master of his craft.

Goldman engaged Leidzén in assisting a number of composers who were being commissioned to write original works for the Goldman Band, particularly if that person was new to the band medium. Additionally, EFG introduced Leidzén to famous musicians such as Irving Berlin (see page 111), and Fritz Kreisler, which resulted in additional income for Leidzén as he became their principal band arranger. Other major figures of the music industry with whom Leidzén worked were Richard Rodgers and Meredith Willson. Another interesting interaction occurred when Leidzén and Robert Russell Bennett both were invited to dinner (1939) with Sergei Rachmaninoff. Rachmaninoff needed advice on the saxophone, an instrument he hoped to incorporate in his *Symphonic Dances*. This contact led Rachmaninoff to request that Leidzén produce a band score of Rachmaninoff's *Italian Polka* and famous *Vocalise*—both arrangements were premiered by the Goldman Band.[14] Other representative Leidzén projects included adapting Miakovsky's *Symphony for Band* for the modern instrumentation of the Goldman Band and drafting Vincent Persichetti's short score for *Divertimento*.[15]

The short scores of Leidzén's (see page 112) showing the first few bars of *Italian Polka* have been hailed as great aids for conductors but they had a practical origin. Band publishers could rarely afford to print full scores in the 1930s and 40s, but the old Solo Cornet/Conductor parts were just not adequate for the more complex band repertoire that was emerging. Leidzén's short scores were particularly well marked and useful on multiple levels.

Both Richard and EFG stepped forward to champion Leidzen's text *An Invitation to Band Arranging*. This book was representative of the work Leidzén did as a teacher at Interlochen Music Camp, for William Revelli's graduate band program at the University of Michigan, for the private lessons he gave in his Manhattan apartment, and his classes at the Ernest Williams Music Camp. The book also stands as a testament to Goldman and Leidzén's philosophy of band instrumentation, including a very forward-thinking speculation on the wind ensemble concept, in contrast to Goldman's larger 'symphony band', nearly a third of which was the soprano clarinet section.[16] While this text was completed in 1946, it took four more years, and a good deal of advocacy and promotion from both Goldmans for the book to get into print in 1950 (published by Oliver Ditson—Theodore Presser Co.). (see page 113)

During the war years of the 1940s, the professional relationship between Erik and

EFG began to blossom into a personal friendship. On the professional level, EFG kept Erik busy with pre-season arranging and composing and also invited him to conduct the regular Goldman Band, or smaller units at special functions. Leidzén returned the compliment by inviting Goldman to direct the Arma Corporation Band and Chorus, an excellent musical organization led by Erik Leidzén that flourished at the Brooklyn Navy Yard.[17] By 1942 Erik and Maria Leidzén began to be invited on a regular basis to Goldman's second home along the Hudson River at Mt Tremper, called *Maidstone*. Leidzén's personal correspondence to his sister in Sweden at this time is filled with detailed accounts of these up-river retreats. By nature, Goldman was a proper old New Yorker and Leidzén had the manners of a European gentleman which still kept their personal relationship on a formal level. However, things changed in the summer of 1949 when, after another weekend at *Maidstone*, EFG wrote: "Dear Erik: I feel so close to you and Maria that in the future I propose to call you by your first names. I'm sure neither of you will mind."

In 1946, Goldman graciously supported Erik Leidzén's return to The Salvation Army, where he first served as a consultant and then editor of the SA's band music publications. Leidzén's next assignment was to train a whole generation of SA bandmasters by offering twelve-week training courses all across the Eastern half of the United States. At graduation ceremonies EFG was frequently an honored guest and would hand out the certificates, add appropriate remarks, and conduct the "bandmasters' band" in one of his marches. EFG lent great credibility to the significant renaissance of the music program that Salvation Army experienced in the 1950s. To the end of his life, Goldman volunteered in this capacity and other ways whenever possible.[18]

Shortly after World War II, EFG traveled throughout the Pacific area visiting military installations where he studied and conducted bands of the U.S. Army. His criticism of the bands was quite harsh as seen in a detailed 'diary' of his findings which read in part:

> Unfortunately I am unable to write very favorably about our Army bands, for I found them to be quite inferior to those of foreign countries. There are many reasons for this, the principal one being that the entire band system is wrong from top to bottom. Under the present system it is almost impossible to develop good bands—or to attract good musicians or good bandmasters to the service.[19]

By 1949, the United States Navy had approached Goldman, William Schuman (Julliard), and Earl Moore (University of Michigan) to investigate the state of the Navy's domestic band program. Schuman called Leidzén and asked if he would be willing to substitute for him, to which Erik readily consented. The three men traveled to Washington, DC, December 1949, returning there and to Norfolk in February, 1950. Exhaustive interviews of both officers and enlisted men were held, bands were inspected, and reports were submitted to the appropriate military authorities and congressional committee. They also traveled to the naval base in San Diego to continue their work. Their reports proved a strong catalyst and support for the restructuring of U.S. military bands, their training program, and the nurturing of quality band directors undertaken by all the services in the early 1950s. For Leidzén, these new contacts meant commissions from the US Navy Band, Air Force Band, West Point Academy Band, and guest conducting appearances with all three, as well as the premiere of his major orchestral work, his 60-minute *Irish Symphony*, first played by the Air Force Symphony Orchestra.[20]

Leidzén's letters at this time are filled with great detail on these travels, and allow for an examination of the growing friendship between him and Goldman. They soon had nicknames for each other. Goldman was "Junior", because he was the eldest, and Leidzén was "Gorgeous Guzzie", from his middle name, Gustaf. Goldman proved himself a prankster and practical joker while on the road, and Leidzén immortalized him in some silly, amusing poems. Letters between them usually had at least one joke. When Leidzén wrote to EFG on 27 September 1948, just after the Goldman Band performed in Springfield, MA he said: "The write-up [on the concert] was favorable…And did you notice the 'slip'? "Jean, joy of man's desiring" is really one for the book." Their friendship had become so close that Erik could write to Mrs. Goldman on 19 February 1950 the following: "Shall do my best to shield Dr. Goldman from the boring sycophants at the ABA-shindig in Ann Arbor. In San Diego he will again be with the compact, efficient and considerate group we worked so well with in Washington and Norfolk."

I have previously speculated about the degree to which Leidzén ghost wrote for Goldman. There is irrefutable evidence that Leidzén ghost wrote a good deal of music for Ernest Williams. However, in the case of Goldman, whenever asked about this, Leidzén hedged and "softened" the observation. Leidzén admitted to my father, Richard Holz (1914–86), former director of the New York Staff Band, and a close friend, that for some marches, he received only the barest sketch, usually just the melodic content. Donald Ross, a student of Leidzén's in 1953–54, saw Goldman march sketches in Leidzen's apartment that consisted solely of a single melodic line. Changes were made to the original tune, Ross attesting to witnessing the 'red pencil changes', and then the harmonization and counter-melodies were added by Leidzén prior to making the "bandstration." Goldman, however, always had the last word, with Erik keeping the marches sounding "Goldmanesque," so fully had Leidzén absorbed Goldman's style.[21]

Several representative marks of the esteem these two men and their families held for each other, both late in life and after each had died, can be highlighted:

1) The Goldman family asked Leidzén to read multiple passages from scripture at EFG's private memorial service, and at the Crematorium. As no clergy were present, Erik acted, in a way, as the 'pastor.' The only other non-family invitee was Vincent Persichetti, who played Bach on the organ.[22]

2) The Salvation Army, at Leidzén's encouragement, presented a

series of Goldman Memorial Concerts and the New York Staff Band recorded a best selling march album for ABC Paramount in honor of EFG.[23]

3) After Leidzén's death in 1962 and for several years thereafter, Richard Franko Goldman and the Goldman Band presented an annual Erik Leidzén Memorial Concert within their Central Park series.[24]

This brief overview of the relationship between Edwin Franko Goldman and Erik Leidzén helps frame and summarize an important period in the development of American band music. Goldman's great achievement in American wind band history was in providing a grand balance in his programming enhanced by an aggressive commissioning project. He highlighted the march, the band's great contribution to world music literature, featured quality transcriptions from the classical repertoire, both past and present, and utilized the best of the light classics, contemporary musical theater, and film music. He also greatly expanded the list of fine original compositions for wind band. In this great achievement Erik Leidzén joined EFG and his son Richard in a twenty-three year collaboration that must be considered among the most fruitful in American band history. Richard Franko Goldman encapsulated all of this when he sent a letter of tribute to Erik on the occasion of a music festival presented in his honor on 5 February 1960, by the New York Staff Band of the SA. In part the letter reads:

> Your long association with the Goldman Band of course constitutes a memorable part of this organization's history. Everyone connected with bands knows of the great esteem which my father had for you both as a musician and as a person. And I can only add that I share these feelings completely. You have, as every musician knows, made an important and permanent contribution to the literature of the band as composer and arranger. We all hope that your activity will continue for many years to come and that we in the band field may look forward to many important compositions and transcriptions from your pen.[25]

Together and individually, Edwin Franko Goldman and Erik Leidzén touched the lives of thousands of band musicians – military, community, school, university, Salvation Army, you name it. The music they produced and our bands and band culture today are richer for what these men achieved.

Edwin Franko Goldman

Erik W. G. Leidzén

Edwin Franko Goldman, Erik Leidzén, Richard Franko Goldman and James Burke, c. 1952.

Page A

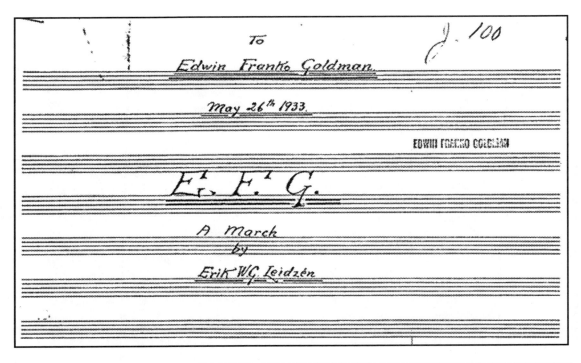

E. F. G. March for brass band.

Top: Title dedication page

Bottom: Page 1 manuscript score

Page B

Leidzén Account Book, 1935–36 (left), and 1936–37 (right) in column listing work for Edwin Franko Goldman.

Page C

```
GOLDMAN
Anniversary March
Score 26 pages á 5:00        130:00
Cond. 7          3:00         21:00

Old Glory Forever
Score 25 pages á 5:00        125:00
Cond. 7          3:00         21:00

Exultation Waltz
Piano 11 pages á 4:00         44:00
Cornet 6         1:00          6:00
                            _____
                             347:00
        October 3, 1941
SMILE FOR ME arr. Band
Pitch Program March 7         50:00

SAVE THE AMERICAN WAY
Goldman, Voice and Piano      35:00

EXULTATION WALTZ arr.
for Band, Score 33 pages     165:00
June 2, 1942.               _____
                             200:00
GOLDMAN
March A 30 pages
March B 22           á 5:00  260:00
Nov. 10, 1942
THE BUGLER Crt and Piano
13 pages á 4:00
Solo part 2 p.á 1:00          54:00
United Nations March
Score 24 p.á 5:00            120:00
December 1942               _____
          /minus 80?//       174:00

March -76
Score 30 p.á 5:00            150:00
Jan. -43 /minus 80?/
```

```
DVORAK /arr/
Old folks at home
Score 8 pages á 5:00          40:00
Goldman
March !!!!!
Score 21 pages               105:00

Bach
ARIOSO              ✓
Score 10                      50:00
Cond   4                      16:00

Moussorgsky         ✓
Love Scene from BORIS
Score 15                      75:00
Cond    5                     20:00

Goldman
The Bugler /Crt Solo/
Score 37 pages               185:00

Timp-part for Shostakovitch
March                          1:00
                            _____
                             492:00

        June 1, 1943

GOLDMAN
March
24 pages score               120:00
March 11, 1944
```

Leidzén Account Book, 1942–44, work for Edwin Franko Goldman.

Page D

Having been employed by EDWIN FRANKO GOLDMAN, New York, N. Y. for the specific purpose of composing the band arrangement of the composition hereinafter referred to, and having received the sum of Sufficient Dollars, ($) as my full compensation therefor, and pursuant to the terms of such employment, I hereby confirm in EDWIN FRANKO GOLDMAN, New York, N. Y., my employer, the ownership of the said arrangement composed by me of the composition entitled

PROCESSION OF NOBLES by Rimsky-Korsakov

and the right to copyright and obtain renewals of copyright of the same, in all countries, and hereby state that I have and have had no right, title or interest in the same, hereby agreeing for myself, my heirs, executors, administrators, widow and next kin, that I will on request, execute such other and further papers, instruments or documents that may be necessary better to secure the said arrangement composed by me to EDWIN FRANKO GOLDMAN, New York, N. Y., and his assigns, together with all rights to obtain copyrights and renewals thereof, in all countries, which I, as the composer, might have had or received, except for said employment.

ERIK W. G. LEIDZEN

DATE

3/23/39

WITNESS:

Agnes M. Fleming

Portion of contract between Leidzén and Goldman for release of *Procession of the Nobles*, March 23, 1938. [Goldman Collection]

Page E

Having been employed by EDWIN FRANKO GOLDMAN, NEW YORK, N. Y.,
for the specific purpose of composing the band arrangements of the
compositions hereinafter referred to, and having received the sum
of   as my full compensation
therefor, and pursuant to the terms of such employment, I hereby
confirm in EDWIN FRANKO GOLDMAN, NEW YORK, N. Y., my employer, the
ownership of said arrangements composed by me of the compositions
entitled

"March to the Scaffold"	Berlioz
Six Cornet Solos	Goldman
"Tango"	
"A Prayer"	
Polka-Caprice "Mercury"	
"An Old Story"	
"Serenade"	
"Country Dance"	
"Sailor's Dance"	Gliere
Overture "Halka"	Moniuszko

and the right to copyright and obtain renewals of copyrights of
the same, in all countries, and hereby state that I have and
have had no right, title or interest in the same, hereby agreeing for myself, my heirs, executors, administrators, widow and
next kin, that I will, on request, execute such other and further
papers, instruments or documents that may be necessary better to
secure the said arrangements composed by me to EDWIN FRANKO
GOLDMAN, NEW YORK, N. Y., and his assigns, together with all rights
to obtain copyrights and renewals thereof, in all countries,
which I, as the composer, might have had or received, except for
said employment.

Portion of contract between Leidzén and Goldman for multiple works;
undated, unsigned. [Goldman Collection]

Page F

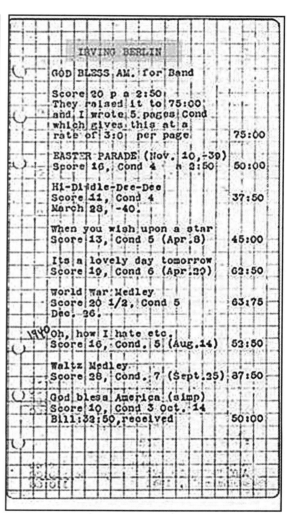

Leidzén Account Book, 1937–38 work for Edwin Franko Goldman.

Leidzén Account Book, page 1 of listing for work completed for Irving Berlin, 1939–40.

Short score of *Italian Polka* (Rachmaninoff/Leidzén)

Page H

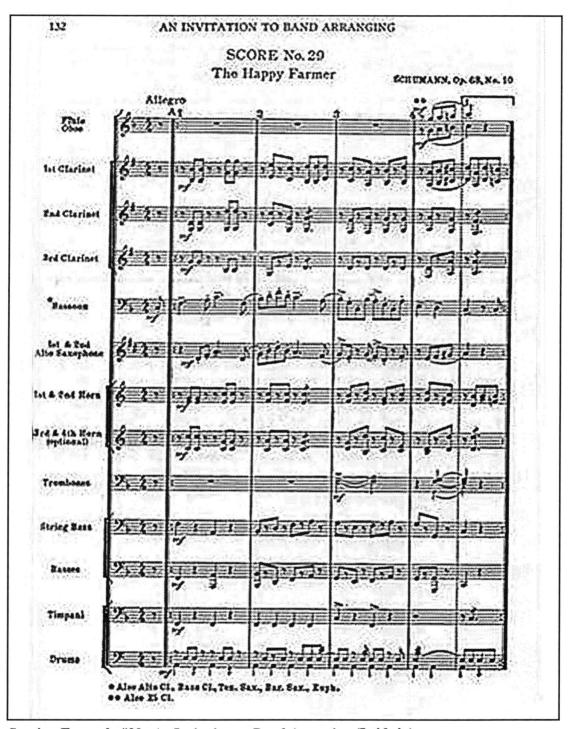

Scoring Example #29, *An Invitation to Band Arranging* (Leidzén)

Page I

Goldman Band cornetists/trumpeters shown with Ernest Williams:
Joe Frey, Leonard B. Smith, Ned Mahoney, Frank Elsass

Goldmam Memorial Concert, 1959: Richard Holz (father of the author),
Richard Franko Goldman, Erik Leidzén, Norman Marshall

Page J

NOTES

[1] For a more comprehensive discussion of the Goldman-Leidzén relationship see the following by this author from which much of this paper is derived: Ronald Holz, "Erik William Gustav Leidzén (1894–1962): His Contribution to Concert Band Literature" *Journal of Band Research* Volume 25/1 Fall 1989), 78–92; Ronald Holz, *Erik Leidzén: Band Arranger and Composer* (Lewiston, NY: Mellen Press, 1990).

[2] The private papers, documents, correspondence, and poetry of Erik Leidzén cited in this paper are housed in The Salvation Army National Archives, Alexandria, VA, Record Group 20.35, herein called Leidzen Papers. There are two account notebooks that survive, catalogued under 221/27 of Record Group 20.35. The first notebook holds accounts for the years 1936—August 1944. The second book is marked on the cover "List of all arrangements made after September 1, 1944."

[3] As a very young cornet player John Allan played with the famous American Band of Providence, RI, before moving to New York and joining the New York Staff Band in 1903–04 as cornet soloist, while studying with Goldman. During World War I he served as chief chaplain on General John Pershing's staff. He later rose to become second-in-command of the worldwide SA. Musically, he is remembered for his excellent playing and for having founded in the early 1920s the first American summer music camp of that denomination.

[4] Goldman's reported words were "in Bandmaster Leidzén you have a man who is a band genius. I say that meaning it and I do not think I have ever said such a thing before." "F.E.T. Ensemble Festival," *The War Cry of The Salvation Army* (Eastern Territory), June 10, 1933, p. 12.

[5] Erik Leidzen's musical manuscripts and personal copies of printed scores – both original works and arrangements – were given to The Salvation Army Eastern Territorial Music Department by his widow, Maria. This collection has recently been moved from the Music Department to the Heritage Museum at The Eastern Territorial Headquarters of The Salvation Army, 440 West Nyack Rd, Nyack, NY. The piano score holding Goldman's commendation is housed in the SA' Heritage Museum, Nyack, NY. The signed manuscript score, with dedication title page, of the initial, 9-part brass version of *EFG March* shown accompanying this article resides in the Goldman Collection.

[6] Edwin Franko Goldman (Erik Leidzen, associate editor), *The Goldman Band System for Developing Tone, Intonation, Phrasing, Books I and II* (New York: Carl Fischer, 1935). Edwin Franko Goldman, *Band Betterment* (New York: Carl Fischer, 1934).

[7] For further details and documentation on the Williams—Leidzén relationship especially the ghost-writing, see Holz, *Erik Leidzén: Band Arranger and Composer*, Chapter 7, "The Goldman and Williams Connection."

[8] In addition to contracts and notebook citations given in this paper found in the Leidzén Papers at the SA National Archives, several related documents and correspondence dealing with Goldman and Leidzén may be found in The Goldman Collection: Special Collections Department, The University of Iowa.

[9] I presented a paper entitled "E.F. Goldman's *On the Mall:* Evolution of a March" at the June 11, 1993 Band History Conference of The Great American Brass Band Festival, Centre College, Danville, KY. Findings from that paper available on request.

[10] Some recent studies criticize Leidzén, R.F. Goldman and other arrangers—transcribers of the 1930–1960 era for not having a late 20th-century aesthetic or philosophy. This is misguided hindsight. We should rather honor them because they were among the first 'modern-era' band men to provide quality performances and editions of long neglected works, paving the way for more musicologically precise versions of the current scene.

[11] The score features both complete sections and certain key soloists, like a cadenza for euphonium with optional double-bell effects for virtuosi like Simone Mantia who liked to feature this instrument from time to time with the Goldman Band. For further details on Goldman programming and commissions, see Kirby Reid Jolly, "Edwin Franko Goldman and the Goldman Band," PhD Dissertation, New York University, 1971 and Noel K. Lester, "Richard Franko Goldman: His Life and Works," DMA Dissertation, Peabody Conservatory of Music, 1984.

[12] See for instance letter dated February 6, 1939, from Leidzén to Goldman concerning *Band Virtuosities*. The tone is both respectful—'Dear sir'—but with a touch of the casual as well, the beginning of a warmer relationship. Leidzén Papers, SA National Archives.

[13] Account notebook, listing for June 10, 1938. $281.00. "This includes 11 hrs a 3:00 [$3.00] for "lessons" for Rich. Goldman." On this same page is the entry for the Rachmaninoff *Italian Polka* as well as several choral—band arrangements of classical works Goldman commissioned Leidzén on a regular basis, including for the 1938 season Meyerbeer's *Chorus of the Bishops*, Handel's *The King Shall Rejoice*, and Haydn's *The Heavens Are Telling*. All of these special choir-band arrangements remain in manuscript and are housed in the Goldman Collection, University of Iowa. See Holz, *Erik Leidzén: Band Arranger and Composer*, Table 6, p. 199, for a complete list. Several of them are designed to be played by either band alone or in combination with large chorus.

[14] The *"Vocalise"* transcription/arrangement was never published, though featured multiple times by the Goldman Band. It is housed in the Goldman Collection, University of Iowa.

[15] According to the account notebook, the preparation of the short score of Persichetti's *Divertimento* was completed October 1950 for Theodore Presser Corporation.

[16] For a discussion of Leidzén's anticipation of the modern wind ensemble (*ala* Fennell) that he projects in his arranging text see Holz, Erik Leidzén: Band Arranger, pp. 125–132, as well as Francis N. Mayer, "A History of Score of Band: The Evolution of Band Scoring in the United States," Ph.D. Dissertation, University of Minnesota, 1957, pp. 322–323.

[17] Goldman once complimented Leidzén on the Arma Band, stating that during the war years it rivaled the Goldman Band. Leidzén used this band as a kind of laboratory, like Haydn at Esterhaza, in which to try out new scoring ideas. Goldman joined in these experiments, frequently being convinced of new ideas by first hearing them tried by this band.

[18] My father, Commissioner Richard Holz (1914–1986), then head of the SA's music department in New York, was the key figure in Leidzén's regained involvement with the SA. Erik first served as editor of the SA's new New York brass publications starting in 1947–48, and then as inspirational teacher and conductor.

[19] A copy of Goldman's "Pacific Diary" is found in the Leidzén Papers. Leidzen frequently edited press bios for E.F. Goldman, several drafts of which remain in Leidzen's own hand.

[20] Leidzén's letters to family members in 1949–50 provide very detailed accounts of his involvement with the military study. See especially December 26, 1949 letter to the McCurdys. In addition to the *Irish Symphony* premiere, Leidzén wrote his *American Naval Overture* for the U.S. Navy Band at the request of conductor Charles Brendler, which was premiered at the February 1951 ABA Convention. He also wrote a short, whimsical *Symphony in the Sky* for the U.S. Air Force Band and, in 1952, his *West Point Suite* for Captain William Resta's series of commissions.

[21] It is very possible that several of the last Goldman marches, including *Wisconsin* (Leidzén listed short and full scores completed April 30, 1955) and *Iowa* (Leidzén listed scores completed February 12, 1956, just days before Goldman's death)) are more Leidzén than Goldman.

[22] For a more complete account of this private funeral see: Holz, *Erik Leidzén: Band Arranger*, pp. 157–158.

[23] This recording was originally entitled *A Salute to E.F. Goldman* but ABC Paramount, which took over the contract from Westminster Hi-Fi, changed the title to a more commercial one: *The Salvation Army Band Plays the Great Marches*. Two Goldman marches in brass band versions, along with other marches by American and British composers, are included: *Kentucky, On the Mall*, as is Leidzen's salute to his friend, *E.F.G.*

[24] Richard Franko Goldman invited my father to conduct the Goldman Band in multiple Erik Leidzén Memorial Concerts in the years following his death, especially 1964–1969.

[25] This letter is one among many presented to Leidzén at that concert; Leidzén Papers. Following EFG's death in 1956 Erik continued to work with his son, Richard, in supplying works for the Goldman Band, though in gradually diminishing numbers. By 1959, at age 65, Leidzén began to scale back the amount of his free-lance arranging, though keeping on the best of terms with Richard and the Goldman Band.

My life in, around, and out of New York—
Like a moth drawn to a shining beacon.
(The Road to New York—a path often and well taken)
by Paul R. Bryan, Jr.

Life is a gigantic pinball game played on an ever-changing board. It has buttons and bumpers that launch us in different directions, and we have limited control where they aim. My journey was launched on March 7, 1920, and by now, I have bounced around for a long time. Fortunately, the uncontrollable ricochets rebounded several times toward New York.

New York has been called "The place to visit, but I wouldn't want to live there" - probably because of its reputation: so many people jammed together- jostling, arguing, competing, and trying to take advantage of one another, or of unsuspecting clods from the boondocks. Be that as it may, it is one of the greatest centers of music in the world. Like the brightest lamp in an open field in North Carolina during a night in July, it attracts and reflects - a beacon, whose light constantly revolves. I have been a fascinated moth- darting back and forth (whenever possible) for some seventy years.

The invitation to ruminate about my connections with New York has provided a challenge. In retrospect, even though I spent substantially longer periods of my life in other places, I am astounded at the enormous influence on my life of people and places between 34th Street (Pennsylvania Station) and 57th street (Carnegie Hall) in Manhattan. I never lived in the "Big Apple" for more than a few days at a time, but the web of situations and of influential people came at my most musically defining times.

EARLY DAYS

While I was growing up during the 1930s, Chicago was, for most "band-men," the center of school-band activity. Living in New Jersey however, I was more aware of New York, (e.g., my family subscribed to the Sunday New York Times). At the naive age of 12, after being conjured by the local Meredith Willson-type music man, I acquired a smelly and brassy-tasting tuba. My grossed-out mother saved her pennies, and determined that it should morph into a shiny silver baritone. It was fun, and my life turned abruptly away from the Boy Scouts.

Historically, during the 1930s, professional band activity was gradually fading as the school band movement was rapidly developing. In fact, Harlan Darling, the band director at Hamilton Township High School where I attended, was a graduate of the University of Illinois, and pictures of its bands graced the walls of our band room. No recordings were available at that time, but I became acquainted with radio's rich resources, especially the regular broadcasts of the great military bands. And, during the summertime, radio station WNYC also carried broadcasts of Edwin Franko Goldman and his Band from Central Park. That was my first view of the shining beacon, and a couple of 'us moths' flew in its direction. The radio also brought the Metropolitan Opera broadcasts on Saturday afternoon, and the Roxy Theater Symphony Orchestra and the New York Philharmonic Orchestra on Sundays. In addition, we constantly heard popular songs like "East Side, West Side, all around the Town," and "Forty-Second Street" from the movie of the same name. No wonder I was attracted by the beacon's enchantment! I still remember my first encounter with the Holland Tunnel, the thrill of finding the Mall in Central Park, and of meeting Goldman and his first baritone player, plus some other players, and asking them to sign my baritone part for On the Mall.

I also remember that they played Henry Hadley's Youth Triumphant Overture and I enjoyed it so much that I asked Mr. Darling if our band could play it. Eventually, I realized that it was one of Goldman's original-composition commissions. About the same time, during the summer of 1934, I discovered that Arthur Pryor and his Band were playing twice-daily concerts in a pavilion on the boardwalk in Asbury Park, NJ. My parents made it possible for me to spend a week there, and to experience, "up close and personal," the sounds of real big-time, professional New York musicians. Pryor and several of his players also autographed my baritone part for his The Whistler and His Dog. Please notice the name of Simone Mantia, one of my revered teachers, on the part.

My awareness of the growing school band movement was dramatically marked by a visit, an opportunity provided by my Illinois-trained teacher, to see and hear the famous Joliet, IL High School Band performing at Radio City Music Hall. They were impressive as they emerged from the pit and rolled back on that huge stage - preceded and followed by the Rockettes! What a show!

Later that year, 1936, when I was in Columbus, OH at the National Contests competing as a solo baritone performer, I was enlightened by the performance of William Revelli's Hobart, IN, High School Band. It was an eye-opener that deeply touched me; and in retrospect, it was music! It became the most important reason I decided to go the University of Michigan where Revelli had just moved. During 1937-41, when I was an undergraduate at the University of Michigan, he was at the beginning of his spectacular career. He invited many visitors from New York to conduct the band, among whom were Edwin Franko Goldman, Morton Gould (we played his Pavane, Tropical, and A Cowboy Rhapsody), and Eric Leidzén.

Another very important up and coming young conductor at Michigan at that time was Thor Johnson, who later conducted several professional orchestras. It's also worth recalling, that the New York World's Fair was invaded in 1939 by Joseph E. Maddy and all the performers from the Interlochen Music Camp, including my contrabass-playing wife and the young future Maestro Loren Maazel, both of whose pictures appeared in a N.Y. Times rotogravure section.

THE WORLD WAR II YEARS

My most important New York "career" occurred during 1942-46. World War II provided me a momentous opportunity: a chance to serve my country and see, hear, and learn from the best musicians in one of the foremost venues of the world.

Less than a month after the attack on Pearl Harbor, I enlisted directly into the 389th Signal Corps Band at Fort Monmouth, NJ, about an hour from NYC. The membership of the 389th included many musicians from New York, such as bassoonist Leonard Sharrow, who came directly from Toscanini's NBC Symphony, and Martin Zwick, clarinetist, later of the Utah Symphony. Other top-notch performers were Herbert Pierson, hornist, and John Krell, piccolo, of the Philadelphia Orchestra, and Russ

Howland, one of the shining lights from the great University of Illinois band tradition. Any notion of my attending the Warrant Officer's School for Army band leaders was quickly rejected.

Thor Johnson ✣

Soon after settling into my new life, I was invited to play in the Rumson, NJ, Symphony Orchestra to perform Beethoven's 5th Symphony. At the reception following the concert, I heard that their conductor had been drafted, and they were desperate to replace him. Recalling that Thor Johnson, my mentor from the University of Michigan, was about to be drafted, I naively called the commandant of Fort Monmouth, General George Van Dusen, who was a member of the Symphony's Board of Directors, and told him about Thor: a highly experienced conductor, who, I believed, was ripe for the picking. Details of pulling necessary strings to bring Thor to Fort Monmouth were never revealed but, two weeks later, as we were returning from our usual noon-day parade, I was delighted to see Private Thor Johnson, who was beginning his two-weeks training right there at good old Fort Monmouth! It was a coup, a win-win situation for all of us. As far as I can recall, the Rumson Symphony gave one more concert, and then dropped by the wayside for the duration.

But, the community was well served as Private Thor immediately went into the afore-mentioned school and returned as Warrant Officer Thor Johnson, the new leader of the band at nearby Camp Wood. "General Van" was, obviously, a very astute member of the 'old Army' and, taking a cue from him, I wrote "General Van March" in his honor. As my wife soon discovered, he was also an avid gardener, and we maintained a great Christmas card correspondence for many years after the war was over.

One of Thor's immediate projects after arriving at Camp Wood was to found the Fort Monmouth Symphony Orchestra. Over a period of two years, we performed a number of concerts with big-time major artists like Zino Francescatti, Dusolina Giannini, Morton Gould, Eugene List, Eleanor Steber, and Polyna Stoska – all with the eager cooperation of their New York agents.

Percy Grainger and Lincolnshire Posy ✣

We also combined rehearsals and performances with Thor's band at Camp Wood. The most memorable was with Percy and Ella Grainger on November 9, 1943. It must have been one of the first to include Lincolnshire Posy. The Graingers detrained at the railroad station, with Ella (who carried the bells for Lincolnshire Posy) walking one step to the rear of Percy. He was wearing white tennis shoes (in the cold New Jersey winter) and carried their clothes in a knapsack on his back. Their little procession was quite a spectacle that elicited comments from many bystanders.

'Posy' was an eye-opener for me in many ways. For example, I had never heard the sound of a complete saxophone ensemble, including the soprano and bass, instruments that were clearly basic to Percy's concept of the piece. If I recall correctly, Thor had been at great pains to see that there was a bass sax available, undoubtedly at

120

Percy's request. The rhythmic freedom, especially of "Rufford Park Poachers" and "Lord Melbourne" was unfamiliar territory to most of us as were the wonderful harmonic richness and astonishing dissonances. Terribly exciting to me was the incredible ppp horn-dominated chord that emerged out of the huge crescendo in m. 35 of "Lord Melbourne." Percy came to Duke University in 1958, and we played 'Posy' (unfortunately without the bass saxophone) along with other of his pieces, and the inevitable Grieg piano concerto with Percy as soloist. I have a number of letters from him and, of course, many stories. He was indeed a remarkable and significant composer, and I treasure my contacts with him, especially with 'Posy.' My wife also remembers the problem she faced in trying to satisfy his vegetarian appetite when he stayed with us in Durham!

Vittorio Giannini

Through Thor, I also met Vittorio Gianinni and arranged to study harmony and counterpoint privately with him in his apartment around the corner from Carnegie Hall. It led to a personal friendship with him and his elegant and sophisticated wife, Lucia, as well as admission into a circle of friends that included Thor. Dorothy Fee, another student of Giannini's, hosted us at fabulous gourmet German dinner meetings in her home in Elizabeth, NJ - a special treat in wartime. She had written the libretto for his The Taming of the Shrew, a first-class opera, and we were thrilled to hear Vittorio play and sing it. Later, I asked him if he would ever be willing to compose something for band. The answer: "Professional composers are guided by the commissions they are offered...," or words to that effect. The implication: call me when you have money to offer. The story continues in post WW II when a source became available.

The Trombone, Cello, and Piano

One of my personal missions was to study with the best trombone teachers in New York. The first was Wayne Lewis, whose store on 48th Street had teaching studios and was kind of a 'hang-out.' There was a constant traffic of great brass performers including Bill Bell whose big double-bell tuba sat at the top of the stairs.

Wonderful Simone Mantia gave me lessons without charge, backstage at the old Metropolitan Opera House where he was the first trombonist and manager of the orchestra. When I attended a performance, I would go down to the first floor at intermissions and look into the pit, where he inevitably was. He would look up, smile, and get his trombone to play a little virtuostic 'all-over-the-horn' solo. It was a great little ritual! Another teacher was Donald S. Reinhart, the inventor of the "Pivot System," and the only teacher who offered technical advice.

And finally, there was Gardell Simon, the composer of Atlantic Zephyrs, who was a member of Toscanini's NBC Symphony. He had created a special short trombone (in D) that was supposed to make it easier to play Ravel's scary Bolero. He tried to sell it to me! Sometime later, I heard (a true story!) that Toscanini scheduled the piece, and that Simon became ill and could not (or would not) play the high and very exposed trombone solo. Subsequently, the solo was assigned to the lead trombonist in the NBC house big-band (Tommy Dorsey-type), who buckled under the enormous pressure. Each teacher, incidentally, had his own line of mouthpieces. The ones I acquired can be seen in this picture [picture of PB's mouthpieces].

I also studied 'cello with Raphael Kramer, a pupil of Emanuel Feuermann, and piano with his mother, Selma Kramer. They were members of an elite group of prominent musicians in New York that included the great 'cellist Piatigorsky and were characterized as the 'Piatigorsky circle.'

For about two years, the 389th's dance band provided the music for weekly broadcasts of "Music from Monmouth." The show was sent from the studios of station WNEW in New York City on Thursday nights. It afforded me the experience of a professional atmosphere and of composing the show's theme song. The traveling back and forth between Fort Monmouth and the city in open army trucks was, at the least, interesting!

Even a train ride into and back from New York could be exciting in war-times. My wife Ginny and I both recall with considerable glee one night in January when the train was filled with tired and instantly-asleep soldiers who had dragged themselves to the train and then collapsed on the Pennsylvania's "Midnight Owl", confidently anticipating their return to Ft. Monmouth. At 11:58 PM, the conductor, with a bizarre sense of humor, caused instant panic among us by announcing an incorrect order of the stations where the train would be stopping. Normally, after Rahway NJ, we would expect to stop at Perth Amboy. But that night, he said "New Brunswick and Trenton," which meant that we were on the wrong train and there was not enough time to get to the correct one which was snuggled up to the opposite platform - across the tracks. Immediately after we all awakened with a yell, we heard his sardonic laughter. It still rings in our ears!

In and Around New York City

Some of my happiest memories come from 'haunts and places' where major musical events were held. The top balcony of Carnegie Hall was the best place to hear the leading symphony orchestras (e.g., the Boston, Cleveland, Philadelphia, New York Philharmonic [NYPO]). And, directly behind Carnegie Hall on 56th Street was Patelson's Music Shop, which sold used and half-price scores; almost every concert was followed by a visit and the purchase of a score.

Other fond memories: Pennsylvania Station and Grand Central Terminal; the subways: I.R.T. and B.M.T.; Radio City Music Hall; the Paramount Theater ("meeting" Les Brown, a '35 Duke graduate-a 'pre-acquaintance,' long before I joined the Duke faculty); the famous Stage Door Canteen; the 48th Street Theater from which Fred Waring (with Robert Shaw) broadcast at 6:00 PM on weekdays; 52nd Street ('the street' for great jazz); special memories of Jack Teagarden, and Vic Dickinson; Times Square and 42nd Street; Chinese restaurants, and Italian restaurants, with those fancy coffee machines after concerts, frequently with Giannini.

A few of the concerts were unforgettable (mostly in Carnegie Hall and made possible by the USO which distributed free tickets that had been donated for service men): The Royal Air Force Band with Dennis Brain; Schubert's Symphony No. 7, performed by the Cleveland, the Philadelphia, and the Boston Symphony Orchestras - all within a 10 day period; an exciting performance by the NYPO, conducted by Artur Rodzinski, of Rachmaninoff's Symphony No. 2 (my first acquaintance with it); a performance by the NYPO of a monster composition by Villa-Lobos when the whole orchestra appeared to be lost; Brahms 3rd symphony performed by Toscanini and the NBC Symphony in Studio 8H; a concert at Lewisohn Stadium and meeting young African-American composer Ulysses Kay, whom I later invited to Duke for an exciting performance of his Forever Free with the Duke Wind Symphony. Also, there was a visit to Vincent Bach's factory in the Bronx in 1945, hoping that he would replace a mouthpiece that didn't live up to its 12C specifications. Bach made a clever decision: he didn't substitute a new one; he merely punched my initials into it. A bit later, he asked if I would be interested to work for him after the war, which was then grinding to a close. Hmm!

NEW YORK EXPERIENCES AFTER WORLD WAR II

Those four years under the influences of New York were equivalent to a special kind of graduate degree, a time of maturing and realizing that a career as a trombonist would probably be beyond my abilities, and furthermore, would be musically unrewarding. I was ready for further study in theory and conducting and wanted to work among colleagues at the university level. So my wife and I returned to the University of Michigan in 1946, a time which coincided with the University's drive to develop a PhD level degree in musicology. My latent interest in Mozart and his Viennese contemporaries was piqued and the new program appeared inviting, so I went for it and have never been sorry.

I taught at Duke University from 1951-88. During the first decade, my responsibilities included the marching and concert bands (plus theory classes). Both bands drew me back to the "Big Apple." We regularly went on Northern tours with the Concert Band, which was named (at the behest of the students) Duke Wind Symphony, and in 1974 were ensconced for the final night in New York's famous centrally-located Hotel Edison, still one of the better "three-star" places to stay. It usually served as the end point for the Duke Wind Symphony's biennial north-bound spring tour. The Edison was also home to a theater which, for many years, devoted itself exclusively to the then considered risqué show, Oh Calcutta. On one of my more memorable birthdays, I was treated to a front row seat in the midst of the entire group! The Edison also provided for our short-short term ad hoc needs at the beginning of our first Program in Vienna. It involved a late night check-in due to a much-delayed and suddenly aborted flight by Icelandic Airways. The incoming plane that was to take us to Vienna (Luxemburg to be precise), had collided with a pigeon (or was it a seagull?), so we were bused from Kennedy Airport to the Edison at about midnight, and returned to Icelandic's terminal at 7:00 AM.. That terminal was the gathering place for each of the Duke Wind Symphony's five Vienna Programs that I led. It too, has for me, many precious memories of both departures: excited students, (and their elated but apprehensive parents); and returns, tired but exhilarated, after a semester abroad they would never forget.

My most spectacular New York memory was with the marching band [the DUMB, i.e. Duke University Marching Band]. Duke played football against Army in the Polo Grounds. To get there we were privileged to travel by train, first-class in Pullman cars, directly from Durham—after which we were quartered in some easily unremembered hotel south of 42nd Street. The football team (100 strong) was, of course, fully staffed with scholarship players, but the DUMB had no financial aid to offer, nor did we have the luxury of an excess of players who could step in when there were gaps in the traditional block-marching unit. My memory of the occasion is re-enforced by an official picture, taken from the top of the press box, showing the DUMB marching down on the Polo Grounds field in perfect formation - with one empty slot. An exclamation point to the story was provided by the wild ride back to the hotel after the game when we were escorted by a four-abreast phalanx of New York's motorcycle cops at high speed with sirens turned to the max. They zig-zagged right and left, so that the sparks flew when their footguards hit the pavement (down 8th Avenue on late Saturday afternoon) dodging several million New Yorkers. When we breathlessly arrived back at our temporary home away from home, the police sergeant proudly shook my hand and asked how we had enjoyed the ride. I don't recall my answer, but I'm sure that my relief, in not having killed or maimed anyone, must have shown. It was, surely, the ultimate New York experience, and I'm sure that my wife and parents (as well as the non-New York students who were part of the glorious occasion) haven't forgotten it either. We won the game, so I am told.

Continuing Friendship with Vittorio Giannini ▨

I joined the CBDNA almost immediately after arriving at Duke. One of my immediate interests was in trying to persuade mature composers to compose serious works for band. At the end of the budget year in 1954, when there were 500 unspent dollars available, and remembering that Vittorio had not rejected the idea of composing a work for band, I called him. He was leaving for Italy the next day, but unhesitatingly agreed to accept that sum for a serious composition that had "length and depth," (or something like that). "I'll call you when I get back in September." When he called upon his return, my first question was "What is the piece?" and he said "It's a four movement symphony." Later, after we copied the parts, he said to me "You send me all the masters, and I'll look at them, and then we'll meet at Brevard" where he was that summer. So I took the score and immediately said to him "Vittorio, this is called Symphony for Band. I know you've written other symphonies, and there's Symphony No. 2 for Orchestra, so why isn't this Symphony No. 3?" He took his pen and, without hesitation, wrote "No. III" on my score. It was, for me, a high moment, because it affirmed that he, an established composer, had recognized my concern about the quality of music written for band, and had responded sincerely.

124

Giannini's Symphony No. 3 is a first-class work, and it quickly became a repertoire piece. It didn't blaze new harmonic, melodic, or rhythmic paths for the aficionados who normally dwell outside the confines of the parade ground or football field. It, however, helped open the ears of many of us. Suddenly, we had serious music that was conceived for band and was challenging both technically and musically to the conductor as well as the player and, of course, to the public. Conceived by a master contrapuntist whose challenge was to produce a work that had length and breadth, it is characterized by the "long line" touted by such revered teachers as Nadia Boulanger, especially in the second movement whose beautiful opening oboe solo could easily open a scene from an opera. Similarly, the extended baritone-euphonium solo in the first movement reminded me a little of the long melodies that I used to encounter while playing "Marcie Sinfonicas" as we walked (not marched) following the statue of the patron saint [Saint Anthony?] during the Feasts of the Lights in Trenton in Septembers - except this melody was of a higher quality, soaring, and challenging to perform.

The response and acclamation of his Symphony (and doubtless the encouragement of his publisher!) persuaded Vittorio to write other pieces for band like the Fantasia, and Introduction and Allegro, both of which contain echoes of the Symphony. His contrapuntal mastery, which I experienced as I studied with him during World War II, is especially evident in a wonderful piece that strangely and surprisingly failed to attract the attention it deserves: his Introduction, Variations and Passacaglia. Published by Ricordi, it might be called a vade mecum for contrapuntists, a virtuoso display whose fugal writing features full expositions by both the saxophone and percussion choirs and ends with a gigantic finale.

The spectacular success of Giannini's Symphony No. 3 helped to stimulate and further encourage all of us to perform new original works. During those years many CBDNA members exchanged programs. I still have batches of them. It was thrilling to see how many of my colleagues had performed Giannini's symphony, and my efforts to commission works from serious composers continued throughout my career.

Norman Dello Joio 🔲

Following the Giannini commission and with the help of a wondrous Duke Music Department benefactor, Mary Duke Biddle Trent Semans, a generous grant of one thousand dollars was allocated by the newly-formed Mary Duke Biddle Foundation expressly for the purpose of commissioning a new and significant composition for concert band. It was a thrilling moment, and I immediately began searching to find a mature composer similar to Giannini, whose compositional style was well established. Vittorio mentioned some names of some of his students, young composers who were very good and who he thought would be interested in writing for band. They seemed too young to qualify to the satisfaction of the Foundation. I talked also to my very-astute friend László Somfai, the leader of the Bartòk Institute in Hungary. He suggested the name of György Ligeti, one of his countrymen who have since been recognized as one of the leading composers of our time, but whose style seemed to me to be problematic for the band medium. My correspondence file also contains several letters including a long one to Samuel Barber encouraging him to provide us with a companion piece for Commando March. His answer was cordial but negative.1

Finally I met Robert Silverman who worked for the music publisher E. B. Marks and through him I was introduced to Norman Dello Joio. Norman's name was familiar; he was a Pulitzer Prize winner, whose fine writing for winds, e.g., in the Airborne Suite recorded by the Philadelphia Orchestra, seemed ideal. His response to the commission was Variants on a Mediaeval Tune. He not only selected the primary theme, "In Dulci Jubilo," but used the eye-catching spelling of 'Mediaeval', a small stroke of genius. His brilliant and expressive setting used all the resources of the modern band, even including a little solo for the much-neglected alto clarinet. Like the Giannini Symphony, it was received with open arms by band conductors and audiences everywhere.

The commissioning of Norman Dello Joio's Variants on a Mediaeval Tune brought me into contact with another set of circumstances in New York. As I frequented the offices of Norman's publisher, E.B. Marks Music, I met Felix Greissle, a distinguished composer, student and son-in-law of Arnold Schoenberg, the renowned leader of the important second Viennese School of composers. Felix told me very little about his career, but I discovered that around 1939, he, like Schoenberg, had been forced to leave Vienna. Later, while in Vienna leading the Duke Wind Symphony and its sizeable number of Jewish students, I thought of Felix many times; he was the guiding light and the editor of Schirmer's University of Michigan blue-cover series. It included Schoenberg's Theme and Variations, Op. 43a, whose first version was composed for band, I presume at Felix's behest. I programmed it several times over the years, with great pleasure, each time with new discoveries. One of the most intriguing was that our performance in Vienna in 1973 was probably the first time the original version had been heard there.

Jan Meyerowitz ▨

The success of these two commissions persuaded the members of the Southern Division of the CBDNA that I was the logical person to locate and persuade an important composer to write a substantial serious work—for the insubstantial sum of $500.00 that John Butler of Clemson University had extracted from the uniform manufacturer Adolph Ostwald. Considering that the latter had previously agreed to make a yearly stipend of $1000.00 available to the ABA to be used as the prize for the ABA's original composition contest, the money was truly insufficient and had gone begging for some time. In retrospect, I believe that Mr. Ostwald thought it wouldn't be possible to find anyone who would take on such a commission. Nonetheless, I persisted. Robert Silverman was again helpful by leading me to Jan Meyerowitz who accepted it. It resulted in his Three Comments on War—the CBDNA's ill-fated and still almost-forgotten commission.

Meyerowitz's work is really a three movement symphony, that now in 2005 -

another wartime - would be especially appropriate for programming. He was a mature and uncompromising composer who treated the concert band as a worthy medium for his musical thoughts. "TCOW" deserves to be performed by all conductors and bands that seek to perform the best-available literature. But, from the outset, its success was doomed. The premiere performance was especially problematic. The extraction of the parts from the score was the responsibility of the members of the Southern Division. Furthermore, it had to be ready for rehearsal so that it could be presented to the membership at the National CBDNA meeting in Phoenix in 1963 - the same meeting that was to feature the first performance of two compositions by well-known composers: Aaron Copland's Emblems and Ingolf Dahl's Sinfonietta. By convention time, Bill Rhodes, who was to perform it with his University of New Mexico Band had received only two movements, so this is all the members heard. As was to be expected, neither the pre-performance hoopla nor the performance itself compared favorably with those of the Copland and Dahl, and most of the members immediately dismissed the piece. The members of the Southern Division grumbled because they had been forced to pony-up money for the copying. It was for me not a happy experience. I hope that Mr. Meyerowitz and "TCOW" will someday receive the recognition they merit. In following years, in reply to my appeals, he enriched the lives of me and my students with two other excellent compositions, Music Hall Rondo and Four Romantic Movements. The former is a light-hearted and exciting piece which appealed enormously to our students. As with "TCOW," neither of them has been published. All are, therefore, with apologies to Sir Walter Scott, "neglected, unhonored, and unsung!"

A different New York experience led me to a beautiful apartment, No. 4 in 1067 Fifth Avenue, just across the street from the Metropolitan Museum. The occasion was a visit to Leopold Stokowski, where I, as chairman of the Conductor's Workshop Committee, hoped to persuade him to lead a CBDNA conductor's workshop.

Like some of the commissioning efforts, that project also was frustrating. Big-name conductors like Stokowski and Max Rudolph were busy all over the world, and at that time, didn't really comprehend us or our mission. I'd like to believe that American orchestra conductors today realize that their incredibly skillful wind sections are the direct result of training in the bands of this country. A perfect example is Joe Robinson, the NYPO's distinguished and recently retired first oboist, a product of the Lenoir High School Band in Lenoir, N.C.

FINALE

So, be grateful for our profession. As musicians, CBDNA members are among the most highly-motivated, best-trained, and influential group of musical intellectuals in the world. Due to the high artistic standards we have achieved, serious composers are welcoming our invitations for commissions. We have assumed a leadership role in the arts, and are now the leaders in encouraging composers from all levels of age and experience to compose serious compositions in all styles - for wind band. History will show that our contributions are uniquely important to our society's culture and the Art of Music.

We must not forget, however, that we are teachers, whose primary responsibility is to enrich the lives of the young people entrusted to us. For many (most?) of them, playing in a band provides their only exposure to serious music. It's our sacred trust to introduce them to representative works from their rich musical inheritance. In our zeal to promote and perform new works, we should also play tasteful arrangements of fine compositions originally conceived for other genres. And furthermore, we should not neglect such 'golden-oldie' original compositions as Henry Hadley's *Youth Triumphant,* and Vittorio Giannini's *Symphony No. 3*!

Autographed baritone part to *On The Mall* by Edwin Franko Goldman

Autographed baritone part to *The Whistler and His Dog* **by Arthur Pryor**

Thor Johnson, Percy Grainger and Joseph E. Maddy

Thor Johnson and Vittorio Giannini

William Bell tubas

Simone Mantia *Method for*
***Trombone,* title cover**

Mouthpieces owned by Paul Bryan

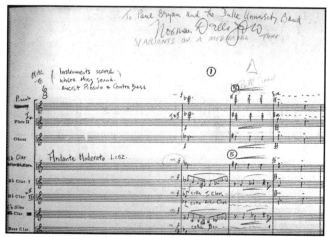

Autograph Score of Vittorio Giannini's Symphony for Band with manuscript III

Title Page of Variants on a Mediaeval Tune by Norman Dello Joio

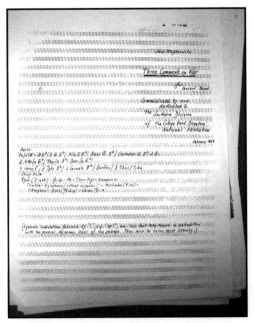

Title Score page of *Three Comment on War* by Jan Meyerowitz

LEOPOLD STOKOWSKI

2 November 65

Duke University
Durham, North Carolina 27708
  Attention: Mr. Paul Bryan
          Department of Music

Dear Mr. Bryan

Thank you for inviting me to participate in your training program
for conductors and performers. Unfortunately for me, I shall be in
Europe during June, July and August of next season, so I cannot be
with you, much as I would have liked to do what you suggest.

                                        Sincerely

1067 Fifth Avenue
New York, New York 10028

Letter from Leopold Stokowski to Paul Bryan